The Ridgewa,

National Trail Companion

supported by

The Countryside Agency
**Landscape
Access
Recreation**

4th edition published February 2006

© National Trails Office

ISBN 0-9535207-7-3

Edited by Jos Joslin & Natalie Kosucu

Photos on pages: Front cover, 4(top), 7, 8,
10, 13, 20, 26, 28(top), 33, 38, 39, 40, 50,
55, 56, 59, 62, 63, 65, 70, 93, 96
© Tina Stallard/Countryside Agency

Photos on pages: 18, 19, 22, 28(bottom),
37, 46, 57, 64, 66, 71, 73, 76, 92
© Jos Joslin

Photos on pages: 4(bottom), 81
© Chilterns Conservation Board

Photo on page 65
© Rob Fraser

Published by

National Trails Office
Environment & Economy
Holton
Oxford OX33 1QQ

tel 01865 810224
fax 01865 810207
email Ridgeway@oxfordshire.gov.uk
website www.nationaltrail.co.uk

Produced by www.leap-frog.co.uk

Designed by Linda Francis

Cover photo:
Downland near Wantage

Contents

I	Introduction	5
II	History	8
III	Wildlife	9
IV	Using The Ridgeway	10
V	Finding Your Way	12
VI	Publications	14
VII	Tour Operators	15
VIII	Useful Contacts	16
IX	Getting There	19
X	Respect the Countryside	20
XI	Emergency Contacts	22
XII	Accommodation, Facilities & Services	24
	Section 1 – Overton Hill to Ogbourne St George	29
	Section 2 – Ogbourne St George to Sparsholt Firs	41
	Section 3 – Sparsholt Firs to Streatley	51
	Section 4 – Streatley to Watlington	67
	Section 5 – Watlington to Wendover	77
	Section 6 – Wendover to Ivinghoe Beacon	87
	Index of Places	94
	Distances between places	95

The Manger below Uffington Castle

The Chilterns Area of Outstanding Natural Beauty

Introduction

87 miles (139km) long, much of it following the ancient chalk
ridge route used by prehistoric man and surrounded by
numerous historic monuments, The Ridgeway offers the chance
to get away from the bustle of life in this busy part of England.
Perfect, but not too strenuous, for long distance use, this Trail is
also ideal for day trips or less. The whole of The Ridgeway can be
enjoyed by walkers with horseriders and cyclists able to use all of
the western half as far as the River Thames at Streatley and
short sections further east.

The Ridgeway

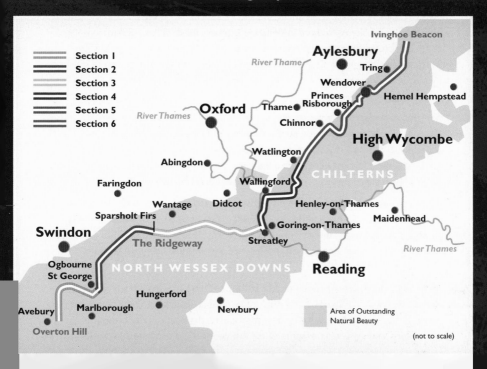

I INTRODUCTION

Welcome to the Ridgeway Companion. It provides up-to-date practical information about accommodation, refreshments and many other facilities along this National Trail. The Companion is designed to help with planning anything from a week's holiday to a short walk or ride.

The Companion is not a route guide: for detailed information about the Trail itself, The Ridgeway National Trail Guide by Anthony Burton (Aurum Press, 2005) is available from most book shops or from Amazon via the internet. Alternatively it can be mail ordered from the National Trails Office (see page 16 for details). The Companion complements the Trail Guide and, armed with a copy of each, it is hoped that anyone using The Ridgeway needn't require anything more. Enjoy your trip.

One of only 15 National Trails in England and Wales, The Ridgeway starts in the famous World Heritage Site of Avebury in Wiltshire. It travels for 87 miles (139km) steadily north east along the surprisingly remote scarp ridge of the downs, across the River Thames, and through the Chiltern Hills to finish in the Iron Age fort on top of Ivinghoe Beacon in Buckinghamshire.

The western half of The Ridgeway, as far as Streatley, can be enjoyed by walkers, horseriders and cyclists, whereas only walkers can use the full extent of the eastern half. Despite its relative remoteness, public transport to The Ridgeway is pretty good, especially to the eastern half, where there are several railway stations close to the Trail and an excellent bus network. With a little planning many places along the western half can also be reached by bus or train or a combination of the two.

The Ridgeway passes through two distinctive protected landscapes, both designated Areas of Outstanding Natural Beauty (AONB). The western half of the Trail travels through the open expansive downland of the North Wessex Downs AONB, whilst east of the Thames it stays amongst the more gentle and wooded countryside of the Chilterns AONB.

In the west The Ridgeway travels as a broad ancient track along the open and fairly isolated top of the chalk downland ridge, often several kilometres from the nearest village. Here, to the south is rolling downland and to the north, at the bottom of the steep scarp slope, the wide expanse of the Thames Valley. The far-reaching views are

6

dominated by the sky, the clouds and small clumps of beech woodland and all you may have for company is a solitary skylark singing overhead or a hare chasing across an adjacent field.

In the past these downs were sheep grazed, but since the introduction of fertilisers in the first half of the last century many areas have been ploughed and planted with crops. However sheep grazing does continue in places and, in others, a characteristic sight is immaculately managed grass tracks, the gallops used for training racehorses. The excellent turf of the downs makes this prime horse country but you need to be up early to see the strings of racehorses exercising.

At Streatley The Ridgeway crosses the River Thames and another of England's National Trails, the Thames Path, entering more intimate and less open countryside. It follows the bank of this famous river along a lovely 8 miles (5km) rural stretch before heading eastwards into the Chiltern Hills. Mostly on narrower paths, the Trail passes through woodlands, many of them beech, over neatly cultivated fields and across chalk grassland nature reserves rich in wildflowers. In contrast to the western half, although its usually peaceful here, you're never far from pleasant small towns or attractive villages.

With the support of the Countryside Agency, The Ridgeway is managed to the highest standards necessary for one of the most important paths in the country by the local highway authorities with a small dedicated team of staff and local volunteers.

Sheep on Pitstone Hill, Buckinghamshire

II HISTORY

For thousands of years, at least 5,000 and maybe many more, people have walked or ridden The Ridgeway, be they drovers, traders, invaders or today's recreational visitors. As part of a prehistoric track once stretching about 250 miles (400km) from the Dorset coast to the Wash on the Norfolk coast, The Ridgeway provided a route over the high ground for travellers which was less wooded and drier than routes through the springline villages below.

New Stone Age men, the first farmers in Britain, left the earliest remains. Their long barrows can be found at a few places both west and east of the River Thames. It was Bronze Age people from later times, around 2,000 BC, however, who dragged the huge sarsen stones from the surrounding hills and formed the dramatic Avebury Circle. There are many of their round burial barrows along the length of the National Trail.

Hill forts built during the Iron Age from about 500 BC until the Romans arrived in 43 AD are also found both sides of the Thames. These forts command the high ground and in several places they defended The Ridgeway against attack from the north.

In the Dark Ages The Ridgeway was a main route for the Saxons and Vikings who fought many battles during their advances into Wessex. In medieval times it was drovers driving livestock from Wales and the West Country to the Home Counties, not armies, who used The Ridgeway.

Until the Enclosure Acts of 1750 The Ridgeway was a broad band of tracks along the crest of the downs where travellers chose the driest or most convenient path. During Enclosures the exact course and width of The Ridgeway was defined by the building of earth banks and the planting of thorn hedges to prevent livestock straying into the newly cultivated fields.

In recent times use of The Ridgeway has changed greatly: farmers do still use much of it as an access route to their fields for tractors and other machinery but its main use is no longer utilitarian but recreational with walkers and riders out for exercise, pleasure and spiritual refreshment.

Avebury stones

The grasslands which occur on the chalk of the downs and the Chilterns are some of the most interesting habitats in England and some of the richest in terms of the number of plant species found. Chalk grassland has suffered from modern farming and much has disappeared under the plough. However those unimproved chalk grassland areas along The Ridgeway, especially the nature reserves east of the Thames, are well worth visiting where you'll find, amongst many other lovely plants, several types of orchid.

Another botanical treat in store for visitors during springtime is the carpet of bluebells in many of the woodlands in the Chilterns, usually in the first couple of weeks of May.

For those keen on seeing birds, The Ridgeway should not disappoint you. A range of relatively common birds such as warblers and finches are found the length of The Ridgeway enjoying the food supply provided by the hedges lining the Trail. Skylarks, yellowhammers and corn buntings are particularly characteristic of the downland and although generally in decline in Britain are still fairly numerous along The Ridgeway. The song of the corn bunting, likened to the sound of a jangle of keys, is the distinctive sound of the western half of The Ridgeway.

In colder months flocks of redwing and fieldfare, winter visitors from Scandinavia, are common and are usually seen feeding in the fields surrounding the Trail. However, most people will especially cherish the site of a red kite and you'll be unlucky if you don't see one in the Chiltern Hills. These magnificent birds of prey recognised by their forked tail were reintroduced to this area in the late 1980s and are now well established. In woodlands of this area too, woodpeckers and nuthatches may well be spotted.

Apart from the ubiquitous rabbit, hares and deer are the larger wild animals you may encounter. Hares are found in open countryside and are bigger than rabbits with longer ears and hind legs. They are solitary animals and most active at night, so late evening or early morning are the best times to see them. Two species of deer are found on The Ridgeway, roe and fallow with the former being the smaller and also living in smaller groups of just three or four animals. Both of these species are nocturnal and shy so, as for hares, being on The Ridgeway at dusk or dawn will give you the best chance of viewing them.

IV USING THE RIDGEWAY

The Ridgeway provides excellent walking, cycling and horse riding opportunities although it is only walkers who can use the whole length of the Trail.

Cyclists and Horseriders

Riders, both cyclists and horseriders, can share The Ridgeway with walkers all the way from the start at Overton Hill near Avebury to Streatley on the River Thames, a distance of roughly 43 miles (68km). Once across the river the only long section of the Trail which can be ridden is the 8 miles (13km) stretch which follows the Icknield Way through the Chilterns from Britwell Hill near Watlington to Wainhill on the Oxfordshire/Buckinghamshire border. In other places The Ridgeway is a footpath and it is a trespass offence to ride on a footpath without the permission of the landowner.

However an alternative for riders is to join the Swan's Way long distance bridleway at Goring-on-Thames, just across the river from Streatley, and to follow this mostly on The Ridgeway to Bledlow west of Princes Risborough (here the Swan's Way turns north). From Bledlow riders can pick up the Icknield Way Riders' Route which provides a good alternative to The Ridgeway for riders as far as Pitstone Hill, just a couple of kilometres from Ivinghoe Beacon. Unfortunately riders can't continue to Ivinghoe Beacon, the official end of the National Trail, since the route to it is on footpaths.

Vehicles

Recreational vehicles have been legally allowed to use most of the western half of The Ridgeway and a few sections east of the Thames all year round until recently. Now however they are banned from using the Trail (apart from a short stretch just after it crosses the M4) for 7 months of the year from the beginning of October until the end of April. But if you visit in the summer be prepared to see the odd motorbike or four-wheel drive as well as agricultural vehicles.

10

Code of Respect

A Code of Respect has been operating on The Ridgeway for the last few years to encourage all users to act responsibly to conserve the Trail and to be aware and considerate of the rights of others. Details of the Code are shown on page 21 and you are asked to familiarise yourself with it before visiting The Ridgeway.

Be prepared!

- Carry warm and waterproof clothing as even on some summer days wind and rain can make a walk or ride uncomfortable.

- Walkers should wear strong, comfortable footwear. During the summer trainers are usually OK for a walk on The Ridgeway, but during wet periods and winter months don walking boots or even Wellingtons if you're comfortable walking in these. Take a blister repair kit, just in case.

- Wear protection (hat and lotion) against the sun during the summer – the western half of the Trail is particularly exposed.

- Carry water if walking or riding for more than a couple of hours – water points west of the River Thames are relatively infrequent.

- If your walk or ride is along unfamiliar paths don't forget your map and/or guidebook!

 ## Dog Matters

If you are planning to undertake a long distance walk along The Ridgeway with your dog, you are advised to ensure it is fit before you start; on occasions walkers have had to abandon a walk because their dogs can't keep up!

Please also make sure your dog is under close control at all times to prevent it from disturbing livestock or wildlife. You are asked to keep your dog on a lead when you're in the few fields you'll encounter with livestock, although if you find that cattle seriously harass you because of the dog, it may be wise to let it off the lead.

Signing

The Ridgeway follows a series of well-signed public rights of way along which people have legal right of access.

An acorn, the symbol of Britain's National Trails, is used to guide your journey by marking the route in a variety of ways. It is used in conjunction with coloured arrows or the words 'footpath', 'bridleway' or 'byway' to indicate who can use a particular right of way.

The word 'footpath' and/or a yellow arrow indicates a path for use by walkers only and where, without the landowner's permission, it is illegal to cycle, ride a horse or drive a vehicle.

The word 'bridleway' and/or a blue arrow indicates a path which can be used by walkers, horseriders and cyclists but where, without the landowner's permission, it is illegal to drive any vehicle.

The word 'byway' and/or a red arrow indicates a right of way which can be legally used by walkers, horseriders, cyclists and motorists.

The Ridgeway is signposted where it crosses roads and other rights of way using mostly recycled plastic materials. Elsewhere, waymark discs with acorns and coloured arrows are used on gates and waymark posts.

Guides

The Ridgeway National Trail Guide by Anthony Burton, Aurum Press 2005, costing £12.99 is the official guide with written route description and colour 1:25 000 maps.

Harvey Maps publish **Ridgeway**, a detailed waterproof map at the scale of 1:40 000 of the entire National Trail which includes locations of facilities and services close to the Trail. It costs £8.95.

Maps

It is usually a good idea to use maps when walking, particularly in unfamiliar areas. The National Trail Guide includes colour sections of all the appropriate 1:25 000 Ordnance Survey maps needed to follow The Ridgeway. Alternatively, for you to enjoy and interpret the wider landscape, you may wish to purchase your own Ordnance Survey maps.

The Landranger series (pink cover at 1:50 000 or 2cm to 1km) has all public rights of way, viewpoints, tourist information and selected places of interest marked on them. For the whole of The Ridgeway you will need:

173	Swindon and Devizes
174	Newbury and Wantage
175	Reading and Windsor
165	Aylesbury and Leighton Buzzard

The larger scale Explorer series (orange cover at 1:25 000 or 4cm to 1km) has more detail including fence lines which can be very helpful when following rights of way, recreational routes and greater tourist information. For the whole of The Ridgeway you will need:

157	Marlborough and Savernake Forest
170	Abingdon, Wantage and Vale of White Horse
171	Chiltern Hills West
181	Chiltern Hills North

VI PUBLICATIONS

Publications About The Ridgeway

The Ridgeway National Trail Guide by Anthony Burton, Aurum Press 2005 - the official guide with written route description from Overton Hill to Ivinghoe Beacon and colour 1:25 000 maps. Available from the National Trails Office.

Ridgeway, Harvey Maps, 2003 - 1:40 000 scale waterproof map of the entire route of The Ridgeway including information on a range of facilities along the Trail. Available from the National Trails Office.

Exploring the Ridgeway by Alan Charles, Countryside Books, updated 2000 - based on 14 circular walks covering the whole length of The Ridgeway from Ivinghoe Beacon to Overton Hill.

The Oldest Road - an Exploration of the Ridgeway by J R L Anderson with photographs by Fay Godwin, Wildwood House, 1975. Paperback edition by Whittet Books, 1992.

Walking in Britain, Lonely Planet, 2001 - includes a description of the western half of The Ridgeway.

The Greater Ridgeway by Ray Quinlan, Cicerone, 2003. Describes a route from Lyme Regis to Hunstanton, including The Ridgeway National Trail.

Ridgeway Information (Heritage) Pack - leaflets about the history and wildlife of The Ridgeway. Available from the National Trails Office.

Walks around The Ridgeway Pack - leaflets describing circular and other walks from The Ridgeway. Available from the National Trails Office.

Riding Routes around The Ridgeway Pack - leaflets describing circular rides from The Ridgeway. Available from the National Trails Office.

Let's Hear it for The Ridgeway! by Elizabeth Newbery - a family activity book full of ideas and information on things to do and see on and close to The Ridgeway. Available from the National Trails Office.

Ridgeway Public Transport Leaflet - details of bus and train services for the whole Trail. Free from the National Trails Office.

Events Programme - a range of guided events around The Ridgeway. Free from the National Trails Office.

The following companies offer self-guided or guided holiday packages on part or all of The Ridgeway.

Walking

Contours Walking Holidays, Gramyre, 3 Berrier Road, Greystoke, CA11 0UB. **T**: 01768 480451 www.contours.co.uk - 7-night self-guided package from £350.

Explore Britain, 6 George St, Ferryhill DL17 0DT. **T**: 01740 650900 www.xplorebritain.com - 9-night self-guided package from £606.

Freedom Walking Holidays, 4 Almond Court, Swanpool, Lincoln LN6 0HD. **T**: 01522 684104 www.freedom-walking.co.uk

Cycling

Cycling Adventure Tours, Flat 4, Lexham Gardens, Kensington, London W8 5JB **T**: 020 7835 0288 www.venturetours.co.uk - free Sunday rides programme and a variety of holidays, sometimes including The Ridgeway.

Rough Tracks, Alexandra Road, Frome BA11 1LX. **T**: 07000 560749 www.rough-tracks.co.uk - weekend guided tour in Wiltshire including part of The Ridgeway.

Horse Riding

Pewsey Vale Riding Centre, Church Farm, Stanton St Bernard, Marlborough SN8 4LJ **T**: 01672 851400 - www.pewseyvaleridingcentre.com - 1 or 2-day ride from Pewsey to Streatley.

Bridle Rides Ltd, PO Box 9223, Bromsgrove B60 1PF. **T**: 0121 445 6998 www.bridlerides.co.uk - 2-5 day rides along the western half of The Ridgeway for those riding their own horse.

Please note for those visiting The Ridgeway independently many of the accommodation providers listed in this guide are willing to collect you from and return you to The Ridgeway. Many will also transport your luggage to your next night's accommodation.

VIII USEFUL CONTACTS

The Ridgeway Managers

Margaret Caddick and Jos Joslin, National Trails Office, Environment & Economy, Holton, Oxford OX33 1QQ. **T**: 01865 810224. **F**: 01865 810207.
E: Nationaltrails@oxfordshire.gov.uk

Highway Authorities responsible for public rights of way

Buckinghamshire County Council, Rights of Way, County Hall, Walton Street, Aylesbury HP20 1UY. **T**: 01296 382171 www.buckscc.gov.uk

Hertfordshire County Council, Planning and Environment, County Hall, Hertford SG13 8DN. **T**: 01992 555262 www.hertscc.gov.uk

Oxfordshire County Council, Countryside Service, Environment and Economy, Holton, Oxford OX33 1QQ. **T**: 01865 810226 www.oxfordshire.gov.uk

Swindon Borough Council, Highways Department, Premier House, Station Road, Swindon SN1 1TZ. **T**: 01793 463000 www.swindon.gov.uk

West Berkshire Council, Countryside and Environment, Faraday Road, Newbury RG14 5LD. **T**: 01635 42400 www.westberks.gov.uk

Wiltshire County Council, Dept of Environmental Services, County Hall, Trowbridge, Wilts BA14 8JN. **T**: 01225 713000 www.wiltshire.gov.uk

Agency responsible for National Trails

Countryside Agency, South East and London Region, 20th Floor, Portland House, Stag Place, London SW1E 5RS. **T**: 0207 932 5800 www.countryside.gov.uk

Areas of Outstanding Natural Beauty

North Wessex Downs AONB Office, Denford Manor, Hungerford RG17 0UN.
T: 01488 685440 www.northwessexdowns.org.uk

Chilterns Conservation Board, The Lodge, Station Road, Chinnor, OX39 4HA
T: 01844 355500 www.chilternsaonb.org

Organisations for walkers

Backpackers Club, **E**: inforequest@backpackersclub.co.uk
www.backpackersclub.co.uk

Long Distance Walkers Association, Membership Secretary, 63, Yockley Close, Camberley GU15 1QQ **E**: secretary@lwda.org.uk www.ldwa.org.uk

Oxford Fieldpaths Society, c/o Membership Secretary, 28 Harpes Road, Oxford OX2 7QL. **T**: 01865 553699 www.ofs.org.uk

Ramblers Association, 2nd Floor, Camelford House, 87-90 Albert Embankment, London SE1 7TW **T**: 020 7339 8500 www.ramblers.org.uk

Organisations for cyclists

British Cycling Federation, National Cycling Centre, Stuart Street, Manchester M11 4DQ. **T**: 0870 8712000 **E**: info@britishcycling.org.uk www.bcf.uk.com

Cyclists Touring Club (Off-Road), 69 Meadrow, Godalming GU7 3HS. **T**: 0870 873 0060 **E**: cycling@ctc.org.uk www.ctc.org.uk

Sustrans, 2 Cathedral Square, College Green, Bristol BS1 5DD. **T**: 0117 926 8893 **E**: info@sustrans.org.uk www.sustrans.org.uk

Organisations for horseriders

British Horse Society, Stoneleigh Deer Park, Kenilworth CV8 2XZ.
T: 0870 120 2244 **E**: enquiry@bhs.org.uk www.bhs.org.uk

Byways & Bridleways Trust, PO Box 117, Newcastle upon Tyne NE3 5YT.
www.bbtrust.org.uk

Endurance GB, National Agricultural Centre, Stoneleigh Park, Kenilworth CV8 2RP.
T: 02476 698863 **E**: enquiries@endurancegb.co.uk www.endurancegb.co.uk

Other organisations

Berkshire, Buckinghamshire & Oxfordshire Wildlife Trust, The Lodge, 1 Armstrong Road, Littlemore, Oxford OX4 4XT. **T**: 01865 775476 **E**: bbowt@cix.co.uk www.bbowt.org.uk

Chiltern Society, White Hill Centre, Chesham, HP5 1AG. **T**: 01494 771250 **E**: office@chilternsociety.org.uk www.chilternsociety.org.uk

Friends of the Ridgeway, c/o Mr Peter Gould, 18 Hampton Park, Bristol BS6 6LH. **E**: Ridgewayfriends@aol.com www.ridgewayfriends.org.uk

Herts & Middlesex Wildlife Trust, Grebe House, St Michael's Street, St Albans AL3 4SN. **T**: 01727 858901 **E**: info@hmwt.org www.wildlifetrust.org.uk/herts

Wiltshire Wildlife Trust, Elm Tree Court, Long Street, Devizes, SN10 1NJ. **T**: 01380 725670 **E**: info@wiltshirewildlife.org www.wiltshirewildlife.org

From Lodge Hill, southwest of Princes Risborough

Getting to The Ridgeway by public transport is fairly easy, particularly the eastern half of the Trail, and a useful map-based leaflet showing relevant public transport routes is available free from the National Trails Office (see page 16 for details).

Alternatively, telephone numbers and websites to find out more about public transport to the Trail are listed below:

• Rail Services   08457 484950 (24 hours a day)
                    www.nationalrail.co.uk

• Bus Services   0870 6082608
                    www.traveline.org.uk

Information about taxi services is included in each of the six sections.

Those wishing to travel to The Ridgeway by car are asked to park considerately if parking in villages on or close to the Trail. Other places to park are listed within each section.

X RESPECT THE COUNTRYSIDE

• **Be safe – plan ahead and follow any signs**

Even when going out locally, it's best to get the latest information about where and when you can go. Follow advice and local signs, and be prepared for the unexpected.

• **Leave gates and property as you find them**

Please respect the working life of the countryside, as our actions can affect people's livelihoods, our heritage, and the safety and welfare of animals and ourselves.

• **Protect plants and animals, and take your litter home**

We have a responsibility to protect our countryside now and for future generations, so make sure you don't harm animals, birds, plants or trees.

• **Keep your dog under close control**

The countryside is a great place to exercise dogs, but it's every owner's duty to make sure their dog is not a danger or nuisance to farm animals, wildlife or other people.

• **Consider other people**

Showing consideration and respect for other people makes the countryside a pleasant environment for everyone – at home, at work and at leisure.

For further details visit www.countrysideaccess.gov.uk

The downs near Wantage

Code of Respect

To respect this National Trail so that it can be enjoyed by all, please ...

- **Act responsibly to conserve The Ridgeway**
- **Be aware and considerate of the rights of others**

FOR RECREATION YOU CAN	Who
Use all The Ridgeway	(walker)
Use all except footpath sections	(cyclist) (horserider)
Use all except footpath and bridleway sections	(carriage driver) (motorcyclist) (four-wheeled vehicle)

CODE OF RESPECT – YOU SHOULD	Who
Understand that others have legitimate access to many sections	(walker) (cyclist) (horserider) (carriage driver) (motorcyclist) (four-wheeled) (agricultural)
Spread the message about responsible care	(walker) (cyclist) (horserider) (carriage driver) (motorcyclist) (four-wheeled) (agricultural)
Follow the Country Code	(walker) (cyclist) (horserider) (carriage driver) (motorcyclist) (four-wheeled) (agricultural)
Limit your use when the surface is vulnerable during and after wet weather	(horserider) (carriage driver) (motorcyclist) (four-wheeled) (agricultural)
Avoid using The Ridgeway if you can find or develop another route	(agricultural)
Keep to well-used parts of the track to prevent damage to the whole width	(motorcyclist) (four-wheeled) (agricultural)
Continue to help by reinstating the surface where possible	(agricultural)
Make sure you and your vehicle are fully road-legal	(motorcyclist) (four-wheeled)
Make sure your bicycle is roadworthy	(cyclist)
Drive at a quiet and careful speed with no more than 4 four-wheeled vehicles or 8 motorcycles in any one group	(motorcyclist) (four-wheeled)
Ride at a safe and controlled pace	(cyclist) (horserider)
Help other users and make your own visit more enjoyable by using The Ridgeway when it is less busy	(motorcyclist) (four-wheeled)
Warn walkers of your approach and pass carefully	(horserider) (carriage driver)
Warn walkers and horseriders of your approach and give way to them	(cyclist)
Give way to horseriders	(walker) (cyclist)
Watch out for and respect temporary voluntary restraint signs and report registration numbers of those who break codes to LARA (Motoring Organisations' Land Access & Recreation Association). Tel: 01630 657627	(motorcyclist) (four-wheeled)

KEY

(walker icon)	walker
(cyclist icon)	cyclist
(horserider icon)	horserider
(carriage driver icon)	carriage driver
(motorcyclist icon)	motorcyclist
(four-wheeled vehicle icon)	driver - recreational four wheeled vehicle
(agricultural vehicle icon)	driver - agricultural vehicle

XI EMERGENCY CONTACTS

In emergency dial 999 and ask for the service required.

Police

To contact local police stations, telephone the number relevant to the section/county you are in and ask to be put through to the nearest police station.

Section	County	Tel Number
1	Wiltshire	01380 735735
2	Wiltshire	01380 735735
	Oxfordshire	08458 505505
3	Oxfordshire & Berkshire	08458 505505
4	Oxfordshire	08458 505505
5	Oxfordshire & Buckinghamshire	08458 505505
6	Buckinghamshire	08458 505505
	Hertfordshire	08458 3300222

Grim's Ditch east of Wallingford during Spring

Hospitals

The following hospitals with casualty departments are located in the places shown below. The telephone numbers given are the hospital switchboard; ask to be put through to Accident and Emergency Reception.

◆ Full 24-hour emergency service

▼ Minor injuries only, 24-hour service

▲ Minor injuries only, NOT 24-hour service

Section	Town	Telephone No	Address
1	▲ Devizes	01380 723511	Devizes Community Hospital, New Park Road, Devizes (daily 8am-10pm)
	▲ Marlborough	01672 517200	Savernake Hospital, London Road, Marlborough (daily 8am-10pm)
	◆ Swindon	01793 604020	The Great Western Hospital, Marlborough Road, Swindon
2	◆ Swindon	01793 604020	The Great Western Hospital, Marlborough Road, Swindon)
	▲ Marlborough	01672 517200	Savernake Hospital, London Road, Marlborough (daily 8am-10pm)
3	▲ Wallingford	01491 208500	Wallingford Community Hospital, Reading Road, Wallingford (daily 9am-5pm)
4	▲ Wallingford	01491 208500	Wallingford Community Hospital, Reading Road, Wallingford (daily 9am-5pm)
5	◆ Aylesbury	01296 315000	Stoke Mandeville Hospital, Mandeville Road, Aylesbury
6	◆ Aylesbury	01296 315000	Stoke Mandeville Hospital, Mandeville Road, Aylesbury

XII ACCOMMODATION, FACILITIES & SERVICES

This booklet gives details of the settlements, accommodation, eating places, shops, attractions and other facilities along The Ridgeway. They are listed in geographic order from Overton Hill to Ivinghoe Beacon.

If you fail to find accommodation using this guide please contact the Tourist Information Centres listed near the beginning of each section which may be able to provide other addresses.

The Ridgeway is divided into six sections as indicated on the map on page 5. At the start of each section is a map showing the settlements close to the Trail within that section. These maps are meant only as a guide and you are recommended to use this Companion in conjunction with The Ridgeway National Trail Guide or maps.

You are strongly advised to book accommodation in advance. Whilst booking, do check prices since those quoted here are usually the minimum charged.

For those who would like to enjoy more than a day on The Ridgeway without having to carry all their possessions, many accommodation providers have indicated whether they are willing to transport the luggage you don't need during the day to your next night's accommodation. The fee charged for this service needs to be discussed and agreed at the time of the booking. Accommodation providers have also indicated if they are willing to collect you from The Ridgeway and deliver you back after your stay.

All the information within this Companion is as accurate as possible. Inclusion of accommodation does not constitute a recommendation although it is indicated in the details whether an establishment has a recognised grade awarded to it. If you have any comments or notice any errors, please write to Jos Joslin the National Trails Manager (page 16).

Camping on The Ridgeway

The situation regarding camping on The Ridgeway is, in theory, clear enough; The Ridgeway is privately owned and the public right of way along it is for passage only, not for stopping and camping.

In practice, however, most landowners do not object if a tent is pitched on The Ridgeway for a night and disappears the next morning as long as no litter is left, no damage done, nor camp fires lit. Do not camp in adjoining fields, woods or gallops without prior permission from the landowner.

Key to Symbols for Settlements

Any comments relate to preceding icon.

	map grid reference (see start of each section for relevant maps)
	shortest walking distance from The Ridgeway
	most convenient train station
	telephone
	toilets
&WC	toilets adapted for disabled users
	Tourist Information Centre
	pub (usually open lunchtimes 11am-3pm then evenings 6pm-11pm). Names and telephone numbers of pubs are given for those settlements with two or fewer pubs
✕	bar meals in pub
✉	post office (usual opening hours 9am-5.30pm weekdays; 9:00-12.30pm Sat)
	general store (usual opening hours daily 9am-5.30pm Mon-Sat)
	cafe/tea shop
	restaurant
	food take-away

opening hours of services relate to the preceding symbol

S M T W T F S

eg: open all day   closed all day

Post offices, general stores,
cafe/tea shops - open morning;
Pubs, bar meals, restaurants,
takeaways - open lunchtime

Post offices, general stores,
cafe/tea shops - open afternoon;
Pubs, bar meals, restaurants,
takeaways - open evening

£	bank (usually open daily 9.30am-4.30pm Mon-Fri)
	cash machine available, including outside bank opening hours
☆	tourist attraction

25

Key to Symbols for Accommodation

Type of accommodation (symbols in margins)

youth hostel		INN	inn
camping		U	horse accommodation
hotel		SC	self catering

Tom Brown's School Museum, Uffington

The number and price following the symbols for rooms gives the number and price of that type of room available. The same applies to tent/caravan pitches and stabling/grazing for horses. Prices quoted for rooms are the minimum price per room per night for bed and breakfast. The price for single occupancy of double, twin or family rooms is given in brackets eg (£22.00).

Accommodation symbols - hotels, inns, guest houses, B&Bs and youth hostels

🛏	double room	🚲	secure cycle storage
	twin room	**DRY**	clothes/boots drying facilities
	family room		laundry facilities
	single room	🚗	transport to and from Trail by arrangement
🚭	no smoking in bedrooms		luggage transported to next overnight stop by arrangement
👫	children welcome		
♿	wheelchair access	VISA	credit card(s) accepted
	dogs allowed by arrangement	◆	VisitBritain accommodation standard for B&Bs, guest houses, inns
V	caters for vegetarians		
	packed lunches available	★	VisitBritain accommodation standard for hotels
	evening meals available at accommodation or locally		special feature/comment
(G)	grazing for horses		
(S)	stabling for horses		

Accommodation symbols - camping and caravan sites

⛺	tent pitches		showers
	caravan pitches	☎	public telephone
	cold water		laundry facilities
	hot water		site shop
♿	toilets	CG	camping gas
&WC	toilets adapted for disabled users		special feature/comment

Hackpen Hill, Wiltshire

Smeathe's Ridge

Section 1

Overton Hill to Ogbourne St George

Starting in the Avebury World Heritage Site with its wealth of archaeology, this 9.3 miles (14.8km) stretch of The Ridgeway climbs gradually to a high point at Barbury Castle Iron Age fort. From there the route along Smeathe's Ridge provides great views on either side as it gently descends to the valley of the River Og.

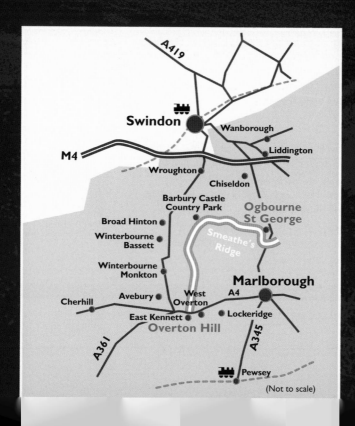

(Not to scale)

Maps

| Landranger maps | 173 | Swindon and Devizes |
| Explorer maps | 157 | Marlborough and Savernake Forest |

Taxis

Place	Name	Telephone Number
Marlborough	Arrow Private Hire	01672 515567
	Marlborough Radio Cars	01672 511088
	Kayze Cars	01672 514556

Car Parking

If you choose to park in villages close to The Ridgeway, please park considerately. Other places to park are listed below but you need to be aware that theft from cars parked in the countryside does occur. You are advised to leave any unnecessary items at home or, failing that, ensure that anything valuable is locked in the boot of your vehicle.

Place	Map Grid Reference
On Ridgeway at the start at Overton Hill, on north side of A4, 4½ miles (7km) west of Marlborough	SU 119681
On Ridgeway at Hackpen Hill on minor road between Marlborough and Broad Hinton, 2 miles (3km) east of Broad Hinton	SU 129747
On Ridgeway at Barbury Castle Country Park, 5 miles (8km) south of Swindon signed from Wroughton and Chiseldon	SU 157762

Water Points

• with troughs for animals

Place	Map Grid Reference
Barbury Castle Country Park (at the café)	SU 158760

Toilets

Place	Map Grid Reference
Barbury Castle Country Park	SU 155762

Vets

Place	Name	Telephone Number
Marlborough	The Drove Veterinary Hospital	01672 512043
	Hayward & Sercombe	01672 514875

Farriers

Place	Name	Telephone Number
Marlborough	J Baker	01672 514013
Aldbourne	Racing Farriers	01672 540812
Aldbourne	Peter Baker	01793 540812
Wroughton	P A Groom	01793 814185

Saddlers

Place	Name	Telephone Number
Marlborough	G & S Saddlery	01672 515665

Riding Stables for Guided Rides

Place	Name	Telephone Number
Marlborough	Pewsey Vale Riding Centre	01672 851400

Horsebox Parking

The following places have sufficient space for you to park your horsebox. You **must** call in advance to arrange as space may be scarce. A fee may also be charged.

Place	Name	Telephone Number
Wroughton	Hackpen Liveries (Accommodation guests and day-riders)	01793 845024
Ogbourne St George	Parklands Hotel (Accommodation guests and day-riders)	01672 841555

Bike Repairs

Place	Name	Telephone Number
Marlborough	Ridgeway Cycle Hire & Repairs	01672 513414
Swindon	Mitchell Cycles	01793 523306
	Swindon Cycles Superstore	01793 700105
	Bike Doctor	01793 874873
	Total Bike	01793 644185

Mountain Bike Hire

Place	Name	Telephone Number
Swindon	Swindon Cycles Superstore (local delivery and car rack hire)	01793 700105

Tourist Information Centres

These TICs are staffed but note that many libraries in the area have leaflets about local attractions and events.
★ offers accommodation booking service

Place	Address/Opening Hours
Avebury	Avebury Chapel Centre, Green Street, Avebury SN8 1RE T: 01672 539425 F: 01672 539296 E: kennet@kennet.gov.uk W: www.visitkennet.co.uk Opening hours: Summer (1 Apr-31 Oct) Tues-Sun 10:00-17:00 Winter (1 Nov-31 Mar) Wed-Sun 9:30-16:30
★Swindon	37 Regent Street, Swindon SN1 1JL T: 01793 530328 F: 01793 434031 E: infocentre@swindon.gov.uk W: www.visitswindon.co.uk Opening hours: All year: Mon-Sat 09:15-17:00

The Avenue, Avebury

Autumn ploughing

Browns Farm

Marlborough, Wilts
Tel 01672 515129

Peaceful farmhouse set on the edge of Savernake Forest.
Ideal base for touring Wiltshire. Immediate access to footpaths & bridleways.
Working Dairy/Arable Farm. Ample off-street parking

2 self contained
properties for
self catering.

Also B&B accommodation: Tea/coffee facilities, some with en-suite facilities.
TV Lounge and large gardens available for guests.

MARLBOROUGH

 **SU1969** 4.4 miles (7km)
🚋 Swindon 11 miles (18km) ℹ

Market town with full range of services, visit www.visitkennet.co.uk for further details.

SC ○ **Browns Farm Bed & Breakfast**

GR SU198678 0.9miles(1.5km) south of Marlborough

Mrs Hazel J Crockford
Browns Farm, Marlborough SN8 4ND
T: 01672 515129 **F:** 01672 515129
E: crockford@farming.co.uk
🛏 2 £34 🥾 1 £34 🛏 1 £50 (£25)
🚭 ⛹ 📷 V 🐾 🚲 DRY VISA

Visa, Mastercard, Delta. Some rooms en-suite

Ⓢ 2 £10 Ⓖ 2 £10

🏠 2 self contained properties for self-catering also available

LOCKERIDGE

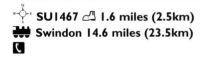 **SU1467** 1.6 miles (2.5km)
🚋 Swindon 14.6 miles (23.5km)
📞

🍺 ▯▯▯▯▯▯▯▯▯▯▯ ✕ ▯▯▯▯▯▯▯▯▯▯▯
　　S M T W T F S 　　S M T W T F S

Pub: Who'd A Thought It Inn 01672 861255

The Taffrail *closed Dec*

Mrs Julie Spencer
Back Lane, Lockeridge, Marlborough
SN8 4ED
T: 01672 861266 **F:** 01672 861266
E: spencer_taffrail@onetel.com
🛏 1 £40 🥾 1 £40 (£25) 🛏 1 £25
🚭 ⛹ (min age over 8 years) V 🚲
DRY 📷 🚗 🦽

WEST OVERTON

 **SU1367** 0.6 miles (1km)
🚋 Swindon 13 miles (21km) 📞

🍺 ▯▯▯▯▯▯▯▯▯▯▯ ✕ ▯▯▯▯▯▯▯▯▯▯▯
　　S M T W T F S 　　S M T W T F S

Pub: Bell Inn 01672 861663

Cairncot ○

Mrs Rachel Leigh
West Overton, Marlborough SN8 4ER
T: 01672 861617 **M:** 07798 603455
E: dm.leigh@virgin.net
www.cairncot.co.uk
🛏 1 £50 (£40) 🛏 1 £25 🚭 ⛹ 📷 V
🐾 🚲 DRY 🚗 🦽 ◆◆◆

🏠 Double room can be made into a twin or family room to suit - call in advance to arrange. Horse accommodation can also be arranged with neighbouring farm.

EAST KENNETT

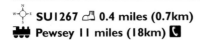 **SU1267** 0.4 miles (0.7km)
Pewsey 11 miles (18km) ☎

The Old Forge   *closed Xmas & New Year*

Mrs L Feeley
East Kennett, Marlborough SN8 4EY
T: 01672 861686 **M:** 07770 871066
F: 01672 861136
E: laura@feeleyfamily.fsnet.co.uk
www.theoldforge.mysite.wanadoo-
members.co.uk
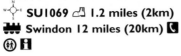 1 £45 1 £60 V
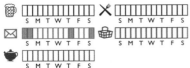 ♦♦♦
Some rooms en-suite

AVEBURY

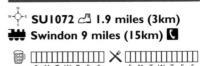 **SU1069** 1.2 miles (2km)
Swindon 12 miles (20km) ☎

	S	M	T	W	T	F	S		S	M	T	W	T	F	S
🍺								✕							
✉								🧺							
☕															

Pub: Red Lion 01672 539266

☆ Avebury World Heritage Site
T: 01672 539250
www.nationaltrust.org.uk

☆ Alexander Keiller Museum
T: 01672 539250
www.nationaltrust.org.uk

Manor Farm   *closed Xmas & Easter*

Mrs Judith Farthing
Avebury, Marlborough SN8 1RF
T: 01672 539294 **F:** 01672 539294
 1 £70 1 £70 (£50) ⊘ ♟
(min age over 12 years) **V**
♦♦♦♦

Avebury Lodge

Mr Andrew Blackall
The Lodge, High Street, Avebury
SN8 1RF
T: 01672 539023 **F:** 01672 539142
E: avebury@email.com
www.aveburylodge.co.uk
 2 £150 1 £150 1 £150
(£95) ⊘ ♟ **V** 💳 Mastercard, Visa,
Debit cards. Some rooms en-suite

WINTERBOURNE MONKTON

SU1072 1.9 miles (3km)
Swindon 9 miles (15km) ☎

	S	M	T	W	T	F	S		S	M	T	W	T	F	S
🍺								✕							

Pub: New Inn 01672 539240

WINTERBOURNE BASSETT

SU1075 1.9 miles (3km)
Swindon 8 miles (13km) ☎

	S	M	T	W	T	F	S		S	M	T	W	T	F	S
🍺								✕							

Pub: White Horse Inn 01793 731257

Broad Hinton

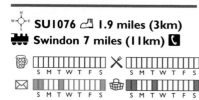

SU1076 ⛺ 1.9 miles (3km)
🚂 Swindon 7 miles (11km) 📞

🍺 |S M T W F S| ✕ |S M T W F S|
✉ |S M T W F S| 🧺 |S M T W F S|

📷 in Post Office
Pubs: Crown Inn 01793 731302 & Bell Inn 01793 731251

Barbury Castle

SU1476 ⛺ on path
🚂 Swindon 6 miles (10km) 👥

🍵 |S M T W F S|

☆ Barbury Castle Country Park
T: 01793 771419
http://193.113.179.211/leisure-barburycastlenaturereserve

Barbury Castle

Wroughton

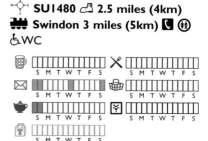

SU1480 ⛺ 2.5 miles (4km)
🚂 Swindon 3 miles (5km) 📞 👥
♿WC

🍺 |S M T W F S| ✕ |S M T W F S|
✉ |S M T W F S| 🧺 |S M T W F S|
🍵 |S M T W F S| ✉ |S M T W F S|
🏧 |S M T W F S|

☆ Science Museum Wroughton
T: 01793 846200
www.sciencemuseum.org.uk/wroughton

Artis Cottage Guesthouse

Miss Kirsty Heather
1 Swindon Road, Wroughton, Swindon
SN4 9AG
T: 01793 845424 **M:** 07974 665529
E: kirstyheather@aol.com
www.artis-cottage-guesthouse.co.uk
🛏 3 £50 🛏 1 £50 🛏 1 £70 (£35)
🛏 1 £35 🚫 ♟ V 🐾 🌑 🚲 🚗 All
rooms en-suite

Hackpen Liveries ∪

Mr & Mrs Glen & Fiona Symes
2 Hackpen Farm Cottages, Wroughton,
Swindon SN4 0QZ
T: 01793 845024 **M:** 07778 103032
⑤ 8 £7 ⑥ 20 £5
📍 Call in advance to arrange horsebox
parking

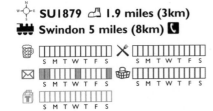

CHISELDON

SU1879 👢 1.9 miles (3km)
🚂 Swindon 5 miles (8km) ☎

🍺 |S M T W T F S| ✗ |S M T W T F S|
✉ |S M T W T F S| 🧺 |S M T W T F S|
💊 |S M T W T F S|

ⓗ Chiseldon House Hotel

Mrs Sue Higgs
New Road, Chiseldon, Swindon
SN4 0NE
T: 01793 741010 **F:** 01793 741059
E: info@chiseldonhousehotel.co.uk
www.chiseldonhousehotel.co.uk
🛏 15 £110 🛏 5 £110 (£90) 🛏 1
£90 🚭 👫 ♿ 📷 V 🚲 🌙 🚴 DRY ☐
🥾 VISA Mastercard, Visa, American
Express, Delta, JCB, Diners, Maestro
★★★ All rooms en-suite

Courtleigh House
closed Xmas & New Year

Mrs Ruth Hibberd
40 Draycot Road, Chiseldon, Swindon
SN4 0LS
T: 01793 740246
E: rhib494369@aol.com
🛏 2 £28 (£28) 🛏 1 £25 🚭 👫 (min
age 1) V 🚲 🚴 DRY ☐ 🚗 🥾
◆◆◆◆ Some rooms en-suite
Ⓜ VisitBritain Silver Award

Norton House *closed Xmas & New Year*

Mrs Sharon Dixon
46 Draycot Road, Chiseldon, Swindon
SN4 0LS
T: 01793 741210 **M:** 07796 750767
E: sharian@clara.co.uk
www.nortonhouse.uk.com
🛏 2 £60 🛏 1 £60 (£40) 🛏 1 £30
🚭 V 🚲 🚴 DRY 🚗 ◆◆◆◆ Some
rooms en-suite
Ⓜ VisitBritain Silver Award

OGBOURNE ST GEORGE

SU2074 ☐ 0.6 miles (1km)

🚂 Swindon 8 miles (13km) ☎

🍺🍴 ‖‖‖‖‖‖‖ ✗ ‖‖‖‖‖‖‖
S M T W T F S   S M T W T F S

Pubs: Inn With The Well 01672 841445
& Parklands Hotel 01672 841555

↺ ⓗ **Parklands Hotel &
Bentleys Restaurant**

Mr Mark Bentley
High Street, Ogbourne St George,
Marlborough SN8 1SL
T: 01672 841555 **F:** 01672 841533
E: enquiries@parklandshoteluk.co.uk
www.parklandshoteluk.co.uk
🛏 3 £75 🛏 6 £75 (£65) 🛏 2 £55
🚭 ‡‡ (ages 0-3 or 10+) ♿ 🖥 V 🏍 🕭
🚲 DRY 🧖 VISA Mastercard, Visa,
Delta, Maestro ◆◆◆◆ All rooms
en-suite
🏅 2 £10
🛑 Call in advance to arrange horsebox
parking

The Inn with the Well 🏨

Mr Mike Shaw
Marlborough Road, Ogbourne St
George, Marlborough SN8 1SQ
T: 01672 841445 **F:** 01672 841056
E: info@theinnwiththewell.com
www.theinnwiththewell.co.uk
🛏 3 £55 🛏 2 £55 (£42) 🛏 1 £75
🚭 ‡‡ ♿ 🖥 V 🏍 🕭 🚲 DRY 🧖 VISA
Mastercard, Visa, American Express,
Delta ◆◆◆ All rooms en-suite

Foxlynch 🏕↺

Mr G Edwins
Ogbourne St George, Marlborough
SN8 1TD
T: 01672 841307
🛏 1 £20/person 🚭 ‡‡ 🖥 🚲 DRY
All rooms en-suite
🏕 10 £5/person 🚐 1 £5/person 🖥 🚰
🚰 ♨ 🖥 🚲 DRY
🏅 4 £10 🏅 2 £10

Ogbourne St George

Racehorses on gallops at Kingston Lisle

Strip lynchet, Bishopstone

Section 2

Ogbourne St George to Sparsholt Firs

Probably the most remote section of The Ridgeway, this 16 miles (25.6km) runs along the scarp face of the downs passing two Iron Age forts at Liddington and Uffington, the Stone Age long barrow of Wayland's Smithy and the wonderful figure of the Uffington White Horse. It also passes the only pub, at Fox Hill, directly on the western half of the Trail!

(Not to scale)

Maps

Landranger maps	174	Newbury and Wantage
Explorer maps	157	Marlborough and Savernake Forest
	170	Abingdon, Wantage and Vale of White Horse

Taxis

Place	Name	Telephone Number
Lambourn	Ray's	01488 71819
Childrey	Berkely Executive Cars	07775 647790
East Challow	Grove Cabs	01235 772200
Letcombe Regis	Regis Cars of Wantage	07748 183381
Wantage	Webb's of Wantage	07881 647777

Car Parking

If you choose to park in villages close to The Ridgeway, please park considerately. Other places to park are listed below but you need to be aware that theft from cars parked in the countryside does occur. You are advised to leave any unnecessary items at home or, failing that, ensure that anything valuable is locked in the boot of your vehicle.

Place	Map Grid Reference
On Ridgeway at Fox Hill near Wanborough, 200m north-east of Shepherds Rest pub on road to Hinton Parva	SU 233814
On Ridgeway 1/2 mile (1km) south of Ashbury on B4000	SU 274844
National Trust car park for Uffington White Horse, south off B4507, 1/2 mile (700m) north of The Ridgeway	SU 293866
On Ridgeway at Sparsholt Firs on the south side of B4001, 21/2 miles (4km) south of Childrey	SU 344851

Water Points

• with troughs for animals

Place	Map Grid Reference
Elm Tree Cottage, Southend	SU 198734
• Idstone Barn, Ashbury	SU 263835
• Hill Barn, Sparsholt Firs	SU 338854

Toilets

Place	Map Grid Reference
Shepherds Rest Pub, Fox Hill (patrons only)	SU 232813

Vets

Place	Name	Telephone Number
Swindon	Eastcott Veterinary Hospital	01793 528341
	The Drove Veterinary Hospital	01793 522483
	Thameswood Veterinary Clinic	01793 511267
Lambourn	RGV Valley Equine Hospital	01488 71999
	The Ridgeway Veterinary Clinic	01488 71505
	Mildenhall Veterinary Centre	01488 72900
Faringdon	Danetree Veterinary Surgeons	01367 242777
	Elms Veterinary Surgery	01367 242416
Stanford in the Vale (near Faringdon)	Christoper Day (Alternative Therapies)	01367 710324
Wantage	Abivale Veterinary Group	01235 770333

Farriers

Place	Name	Telephone Number
Uffington	Mervyn Richings	01367 820253
Lambourn	Chapel Forge Farriers	01488 72613
	Michael Jones	01488 72848

Saddlers

Place	Name	Telephone Number
Lambourn	E J Wicks	01488 71766
Faringdon	Horse Shoe Saddlery	01367 710797
Goosey (near Faringdon)	Asti Equestrian	01367 710288

Riding Stables for Guided Rides

Place	Name	Telephone Number
Kingston Lisle	Holistic Horses	01367 820033

Horsebox Parking

The following places have sufficient space for you to park your horsebox. You **must** call in advance to arrange as space may be scarce. A fee may also be charged.

Place	Name	Telephone Number
Wanborough	Great Moorleaze Farm Bed & Breakfast (Accommodation guests only)	01793 485838
Sparsholt	Down Barn Farm (Accommodation guests and day-riders)	01367 820272

Bike Repairs

Place	Name	Telephone Number
Swindon	Mitchell Cycles	01793 523306
	Swindon Cycles Superstore	01793 700105
	Bike Doctor	01793 874873
	Total Bike	01793 644185
Wantage	Ridgeway Cycles	01235 764445
	GMC	01235 764204

Mountain Bike Hire

Place	Name	Telephone Number
Swindon	Swindon Cycles Superstore (local delivery and car rack hire)	01793 700105

Tourist Information Centres

These TICs are staffed but note that many libraries in the area have leaflets about local attractions and events.

★ offers accommodation booking service

Place	Address/Opening Hours
★ Swindon	37 Regent Street, Swindon SN1 1JL **T**: 01793 530328 **F**: 01793 434031 **E**: infocentre@swindon.gov.uk **W**: www.visitswindon.co.uk Opening hours: All year: Mon-Sat 09:15-17:00
★ Faringdon	The Pump House, 5 Market Place, Faringdon SN7 7HL **T/F**: 01367 242191 **E**: tic@faringdontowncouncil.org.uk **W**: www.whitehorsedc.gov.uk Opening hours: Summer (1 Apr-31 Oct) Mon-Fri 10:00-17:00, Sat 10:00-13:00 Winter (1 Nov-31 Mar) Mon-Sat 10:00-13:00
★ Wantage	19 Church Street, Wantage OX12 8BL **T**: 01235 760176 **F**: 01235 760991 **E**: wantagetic@btconnect.com **W**: www.whitehorsedc.gov.uk Opening hours: All year: Mon-Sat 10:30-16:30

ALDBOURNE

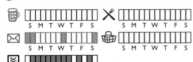

SU2675 🥾 3.3 miles (5.2km)
🚂 Swindon 10 miles (16km) 📞
♿ &WC

🍺 [SMTWTFS] ✕ [SMTWTFS]
✉ [SMTWTFS] 🧺 [SMTWTFS]
✂ [SMTWTFS]

🆎 in Post Office and Co-Op

🏨 The Crown at Aldbourne

Mr Geoff Eccleston
The Square, Aldbourne, Marlborough
SN8 2DU
T: 01672 540214 **M:** 07808 914552
F: 01672 541050
E: enquiries@crownataldbourne.co.uk
www.crownataldbourne.co.uk
🛏 3 £44 🛁 1 £44 (£44) 🚭 ⚥ &
📷 V ⊘ VISA Mastercard, Visa, Delta.
All rooms en-suite

LIDDINGTON

SU2081 🥾 0.6 miles (1km)
🚂 Swindon 4 miles (7km) 📞

🍺 [SMTWTFS] ✕ [SMTWTFS]

Pubs: Sun 01793 790262 & Village Inn
01793 790314

☆ Liddington Castle
www.themodernantiquarian.com/site/3080

Street House Farm   *closed Xmas*

Mrs Elizabeth Dixon
Street House Farm, Liddington, Swindon
SN4 0HD
T: 01793 790243
🛏 1 £50 🛁 1 £50 (£30) 🚭 ⚥ 📷
V 📷 🚲 DRY 🚗 🖐

WANBOROUGH

SU2182 🥾 1.2 miles (2km)
🚂 Swindon 4 miles (7km) 📞

🍺 [SMTWTFS] ✕ [SMTWTFS]
✉ [SMTWTFS] 🧺 [SMTWTFS]

🆎 in Post Office

The Garden Apartment   SC

Mrs Julie Evans
The Bungalow, Chapel Lane,
Wanborough, Swindon SN4 0AJ
T: 01793 791395 **M:** 07973 322163
E: tom.m.evans@talk21.com
www.swindonaccommodation.co.uk
🏠 Prices from £240★★★

Bishopstone pond

Great Moorleaze Farm

Mrs Joanna Rees-Bains
The Marsh, Wanborough, Swindon
SN4 0SW
T: 01793 485838 **M:** 07976 879602
E: joannarees@aol.com
www.greatmoorleazefarm.co.uk
3 £60 3 £60 (£40) ✪ ✝✝ V
🚲 DRY VISA Mastercard, Visa, Delta.
All rooms en-suite
Several £10
Call in advance to arrange horsebox
parking

BISHOPSTONE

SU2483 0.6 miles (1km)
Swindon 7 miles (11km)

S M T W T F S   S M T W T F S

Pubs: Royal Oak 01793 790481 & True
Heart 01793 790080

Cheney Thatch   *closed Xmas*

Mrs R D Boot
Oxon Place, Bishopstone, Swindon
SN6 8PS
T: 01793 790508
2 £45 (£35) ✪ ✝✝ (min age 10) V
🚲 DRY ◯ ◆◆◆

Prebendal Farm   *closed Xmas & New Year*

Mrs Jo Selbourne
Bishopstone, Swindon SN6 8PT
T: 01793 790485
E: prebendal@aol.com
www.prebendal.com
3 £60 1 £60 (£35) ✪ ✝✝
V 🚲 🚗

Cheney Thatch

**Bishopstone, Swindon,
Wiltshire
Tel 01793 790508**

16th Century stone thatched cottage
in unique peaceful setting.
Trout stream through garden,
summer marquee. Heated outdoor
swimming pool. Footpath to
Ridgeway from garden gate.

47

ASHBURY

 **SU2685** ⛺ 0.6 miles (1km)
🚆 Swindon 8 miles (13km) 📞

Pub: Rose & Crown Hotel 01793 710222

☆ Ashdown House
T: 01488 72584
www.nationaltrust.org.uk

Ashbury Stores *closed Xmas & New Year*

Mrs Jean-Anne Schiff
2 High Street, Ashbury, Swindon
SN6 8NA
T: 01793 710262
E: jeananneschiff@yahoo.co.uk
🛏 1 £60 🛏 1 £60 (£40) 🚭 ♀♂
(min age 5) V 🏔 🌑 🚲 DRY 🚗 👫
🚿 Private bathroom available

🅗 The Rose & Crown

Mrs Nyra Karen Stepp
The High Street, Ashbury, Swindon
SN6 8NA
T: 01793 710222 **F:** 01793 710029
www.roseandcrownashbury.co.uk
🛏 3 £55 🛏 3 £55 (£40) 🛏 1 £40
🚭 ♀♂ ♿ V 🏔 🌑 🚲 DRY 👫 VISA
Mastercard, Visa, Delta. Some rooms en-suite

WOOLSTONE

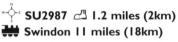 **SU2987** ⛺ 1.2 miles (2km)
🚆 Swindon 11 miles (18km)

Pub: White Horse Inn 01367 820726

Hickory House *closed mid-Dec to mid-Jan*

Mrs Caroline Grist
Woolstone, Faringdon SN7 7QL
T: 01367 820303
E: rlg@hickoryhouse.freeserve.co.uk
www.hickoryhouseoxon.co.uk
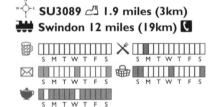 2 £50 (£35) 🚭 ♀♂ (min age 12
years) V 🏔 🚲 DRY 🚗 👫 ◆◆◆◆
All rooms en-suite

UFFINGTON

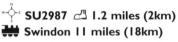 **SU3089** ⛺ 1.9 miles (3km)
🚆 Swindon 12 miles (19km) 📞

Pub: Fox & Hounds 01367 820680

☆ Tom Brown's School Museum
T: 01367 820259
www.tombrown.btinternet.co.uk/
museum/index.html

☆ Uffington White Horse and Castle
T: 01793 762209
www.nationaltrust.org.uk

Hickory House

Hickory House, Woolstone,
Oxfordshire
Tel: 01367 820303

Situated in a delightful village just
beneath the White Horse Hill and
Uffington Castle, Hickory House
offers comfortable accommodation in
a self-contained part of the house
overlooking a pretty garden and
with fine views.

Norton House — *closed Xmas*

Mrs Fenella Oberman
Broad Street, Uffington, Faringdon
SN7 7RA
T: 01367 820230 **F:** 01367 820230
E: carloberman@aol.com
🛏 I £50 🛏 I £65 (£40) 🛏 I £30
🚭 👪 📶 V 🔥 🚲 DRY 🅾 🚗 🎿
◆◆◆
🚻 Private bathroom available

Britchcombe Countryside Holidays — 🏕 SC

Mrs M E A Seymour
Britchcombe Farm, Uffington, Faringdon
SN7 7QJ
T: 01367 820667 **M:** 07748 005362
F: 01367 821022
E: marcella@seymour8227freeserve.co.uk
🏕 30 £4/person 🚐 20 £4/person 📶
🔥 🔥 🅦 &WC 🍽 🚲 DRY 🅾 🎿★
🚻 Mobile homes available from
£120/week. Awnings £3 per night per
unit. Children aged 5 -14 at half-price

The Craven

Mrs Carol Wadsworth
Fernham Road, Uffington, Faringdon,
SN7 7RD
T: 01367 820449
E: carol@thecraven.co.uk
www.thecraven.co.uk
🛏 3 £70 (£40) 🚭 & V 🔥 🅾 🚲
DRY 🅾 💳 Mastercard, Visa, Delta. All
rooms en-suite

KINGSTON LISLE

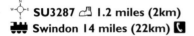

SU3287 1.2 miles (2km)
Swindon 14 miles (22km)

S M T W T F S   S M T W T F S

Pub: Blowingstone Inn 01367 820288

The Blowing Stone Inn

Ms Louise Rainer
Kingston Lisle, Wantage OX12 9QL
T: 01367 820288
E: rainerkaren@aol.com
www.theblowingstoneinn.com
2 £60   1 £60   2 £30
Mastercard, Visa, Delta. Some rooms en-suite

The ancient Blowingstone

SPARSHOLT

SU3487 1.9 miles (3km)
Didcot 12 miles (20km)

S M T W T F S   S M T W T F S

Pub: Star Inn 01235 751001

Down Barn Farm   *closed Xmas*

Mrs Penny Reid
Sparsholt Down , Wantage OX12 9XD
T: 01367 820272 **M:** 07799 833115
E: pendomeffect@aol.com
1 £48   2 £42 (£30)
◆◆◆ Some rooms en-suite
3 £5/person   1 £20
4 £10   8 £5
Down Barn is an organic farm.
Evening meals not available every
Sunday. Call in advance to arrange
horsebox parking

Wescot Lodge   *closed Xmas*

Mrs P Upton
Westcot, Wantage OX12 9QA
T: 01235 751251 **M:** 07730 124888
F: 01235 751251
1 £70   1 £70 (£40)   1 £35
Some rooms en-suite
Private bathroom available

Section 3

Sparsholt Firs to Streatley

This 17.4 miles (27.9km) stretch keeps to the high scarp edge before losing height towards the end as it drops into the Thames Valley. It includes the widest parts of the Trail and some of the best conditions underfoot. This is racehorse country with gallops alongside the Trail in many places.

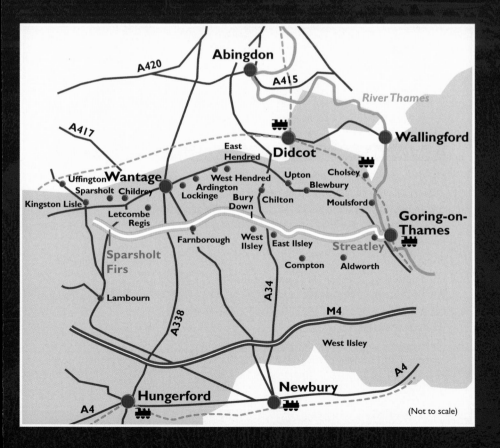

Abingdon
A420
A415
River Thames
A417
East Hendred
Didcot
Wallingford
Uffington Wantage
Sparsholt Childrey
West Hendred
Ardington
Lockinge
Upton
Cholsey
Blewbury
Kingston Lisle
Bury Down
Chilton
Moulsford
Letcombe Regis
Goring-on-Thames
Farnborough
West Ilsley
East Ilsley
Streatley
Sparsholt Firs
Compton
Aldworth
Lambourn
A34
M4
A338
West Ilsley
A4
Hungerford
Newbury
A4
(Not to scale)

Maps

Landranger maps	174	Newbury and Wantage
Explorer maps	170	Abingdon, Wantage and Vale of White Horse

Taxis

Place	Name	Telephone Number
Lambourn	Ray's	01488 71819
Childrey	Berkely Executive Cars	07775 647790
East Challow	Grove Cabs	01235 772200
Letcombe Regis	Regis Cars of Wantage	07748 183381
Wantage	Webb's of Wantage	07881 647777
Farnborough	Gemini Cars	01235 772424
Grove	GP Cars	07799 494847
	Evenlode Taxis	01235 762035
Chilton	Rural Car Service	0800 0743494
Aston Upthorpe	Astons Airport Services	07837 343680

Car Parking

If you choose to park in villages close to The Ridgeway, please park considerately. Other places to park are listed below but you need to be aware that theft from cars parked in the countryside does occur. You are advised to leave any unnecessary items at home or, failing that, ensure that anything valuable is locked in the boot of your vehicle.

Place	Map Grid Reference
On Ridgeway at Sparsholt Firs on the south side of B4001, 2¹/2 miles (4km) south of Childrey	SU 344851
On Ridgeway on the east side of B4494, 3 miles (5km) south of Wantage	SU 417843
On Ridgeway at Scutchamer's Knob, 2 miles (3km) south of East Hendred off the A417 east of Wantage	SU 458851

Place	Map Grid Reference
On Ridgeway at Bury Down on minor road from A34 to West Ilsley (signed Ridgeway from A34)	SU 479841
On Ridgeway at end of Rectory Road, Streatley, west off A417	SU 567813

Water Points

• with troughs for animals

Place	Map Grid Reference
• Hill Barn, Sparsholt Firs	SU 338854
• The Court Hill Ridgeway Centre (YHA), Letcombe Regis	SU 393849

Toilets

Place	Map Grid Reference
The Court Hill Ridgeway Centre (YHA), Letcombe Regis	SU 393849

Vets

Place	Name	Telephone Number
Lambourn	RGV Valley Equine Hospital	01488 71999
	The Ridgeway Veterinary Clinic	01488 71505
Lambourn	Mildenhall Veterinary Centre	01488 72900
Stanford in the Vale (near Faringdon)	Christoper Day (Alternative Therapies)	01367 710324
Wantage	Abivale Veterinary Group	01235 770333
Grove (near Wantage)	Danetree Veterinary Surgeons	01235 770227
West Ilsley	The Cottages Veterinary Surgery	01635 281344
Goring-on-Thames	The Goring Veterinary Centre	01491 873638

Farriers

Place	Name	Telephone Number
Lambourn	Chapel Forge Farriers	01488 72613
	Michael Jones	01488 72848
Challow (near Wantage)	Alf Hall Equine Foot Clinic	01367 710566
Blewbury	Ian Belcher	01235 850029
	Phillippa Jeffries	07887 574112

Saddlers

Place	Name	Telephone Number
Lambourn	E J Wicks	01488 71766
Faringdon	Horse Shoe Saddlery	01367 710797
Goosey (near Faringdon)	Asti Equestrian	01367 710288
Blewbury	Arena Saddlery	01235 850725

Riding Stables for Guided Riding

Place	Name	Telephone Number
Kingston Lisle	Holistic Horses	01367 820033
Blewbury	Blewbury Riding Centre	01235 851016

Horsebox Parking

The following places have sufficient space for you to park your horsebox. You **must** call in advance to arrange as space may be scarce. A fee may also be charged.

Place	Name	Telephone Number
Lockinge	Lockinge Kiln Farm (Accommodation guests and day-riders)	01235 763308
East Hendred	A Monks Court (Accommodation guests only)	01235 833797

54

Bike Repairs

Place	Name	Telephone Number
Wantage	Ridgeway Cycles	01235 764445
	GMC	01235 764204
Abingdon	Behind Bars Cycle Shop	01235 535624
	Pedal Power	01235 525123
Pangbourne	Mountain High	0118 984 1851

Mountain Bike Hire

Place	Name	Telephone Number
Abingdon	Pedal Power	01235 525123
Pangbourne	Mountain High	0118 984 1851

Riders on The Ridgeway above Wantage

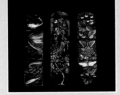

Tourist Information Centres

These TICs are staffed but note that many libraries in the area have leaflets about local attractions and events.

★ offers accommodation booking service

Place	Address/Opening Hours
★Faringdon	The Pump House, 5 Market Place, Faringdon SN7 7HL **T/F**: 01367 242191 **E**: tic@faringdontowncouncil.org.uk **W**: www.whitehorsedc.gov.uk Opening hours: Summer (1 Apr-31 Oct) Mon-Fri 10:00-17:00, Sat 10:00-13:00 Winter (1 Nov-31 Mar) Mon-Sat 10:00-13:00
★ Wantage	19 Church Street, Wantage OX12 8BL **T**: 01235 760176 **F**: 01235 760991 **E**: wantagetic@btconnect.com **W**: www.whitehorsedc.gov.uk Opening hours: All year: Mon-Sat 10:30-16:30
Abingdon	Abingdon Town Council, Old Abbey House, Abbey Close, Abingdon OX14 3JD **T**: 01235 522711 **F**: 01235 533112 **E**: information@abingdon.gov.uk **W**: www.abingdon.gov.uk Opening hours: Summer (1 June-30 Sept) Mon-Sat 10:00-16:00 Winter (1 Oct-31 May) Mon-Sat 10:00-15:00

After harvest near Streatley

LETCOMBE REGIS

SU3886 1.2 miles (0.7km)

Didcot 10 miles (16km)

🍺 |||||||||||| ✕ ▮|||||||||||
   S M T W T F S   S M T W T F S

Pub: Greyhound Inn 01235 771093

The Old Vicarage

Mrs G F Barton
Letcombe Regis, Wantage OX12 9JP
T: 01235 765827 **M:** 07970 567825
E: hugh.barton@virgin.net
🛏 1 £60 🛏 1 £60 (£30) 🛏 1 £70
🚭 🏃 💺 V 🔥 🚲 **DRY** 🔘 🚗 🔆
◆◆◆◆ All rooms en-suite

9 Croft End

Mrs Joyce Coombs
Letcombe Regis, Wantage OX12 9JJ
T: 01235 763694 **M:** 07770 580656
E: joyce.coombs@dsl.pipex.com
🛏 1 £55 🛏 1 £50 (£30) 🚭 🏃 ♿
V 🔥 🚲 **DRY** 🔘 🚗

Quince Cottage

Mrs Louise Boden
Letcombe Regis, Wantage OX12 9JP
T: 01235 763652 **M:** 07989 649680
E: bodens@supanet.com
www.rboden.supanet.com
🛏 1 £60 🛏 1 £80 (£30) 🚭 🏃 V
🔥 🚲 **DRY** 🔘 🔆
🛏 Private bathroom available

The Greyhound Inn

Mr S J Trumper
Main Street, Letcombe Regis, Wantage
OX12 9JL
T: 01235 771093 **M:** 07709 329025
F: 01235 770905
E: thegreyhoundinn@supanet.com
🛏 2 £60 🛏 1 £60 🛏 1 £30/person
(£30) 🛏 2 £30 🏃 ♿ 🏠 V 🔥 🚶
🚲 **DRY** 🔘 🚗 🔆 **VISA** Mastercard,
Visa, Delta. Some rooms en-suite

YHA Ridgeway Centre *phone ahead*

The Manager
Court Hill, Letcombe Regis, Wantage
OX12 9NE
T: 0870 7706064 **F:** 01235 768865
E: ridgeway@yha.org.uk
www.yharidgeway.org.uk
🚭 🏃 ♿ V 🔥 🚶 🚲 **DRY** **VISA** Visa,
Mastercard, Delta.
⛺ Several £6 🍳 🍴 ♿WC 🚿 🚲
DRY 🎲
🏅 4 £10
🛏 Private and dormitory
accommodation available from £14/adult

Harebells

WANTAGE

 **SU4088** 🏕 **2.5 miles (4km)**
🚂 **Didcot 8 miles (13km)** 🛈

Market town with full range of services, visit www.wantage.com for further details. It has a wide range of accommodation and details can be obtained from the Tourist Information Centre - details in the introduction section.

☆ The Vale & Downland Museum
T: 01235 771447
www.wantage.com/museum

LOCKINGE

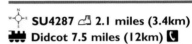 **SU4287** 🏕 **2.1 miles (3.4km)**
🚂 **Didcot 7.5 miles (12km)** 🕻

| **Andersey Farm** | SC 🞨 ⯈ |

Mrs Janine Beaumont
Grove Park Drive, Lockinge, Wantage
OX12 8SG
T: 01235 771866
E: robandjanbeaumont@btopenworld.com
www.anderseyfarmcottage.co.uk
🛖 5 £5 🚐 5 £5 🔌 🐾
ⓢ 8 £21/month
🛌 Self-catering cottage also available from £300/week.★★★★

─── Lockinge Kiln Farm ───

The Ridgeway, Wantage, Oxfordshire ~ Tel/Fax: **01235 763308**
Comfortable farmhouse enjoying a quiet country location,
just ½ mile south of The Ridgeway. Ideal walking /cycling/horseriding.

↻ Lockinge Kiln Farm

⊹ GR SU424834 0.6miles(1km) south of Ridgeway

Mrs Stella Cowan

The Ridgeway, Chain Hill, Wantage OX12 8PA

T: 01235 763308 **F:** 01235 763308

E: stellacowan@hotmail.com

www.lockingekiln.co.uk

🛏 1 £45 🛏 2 £45 🚫 🕇🕇 (min age 7)

V 🥾 🌑 🚲 DRY 🔲 🚗 🐾

💧 3 £10 🔆 6 £5

⚑ Double room can be used as a family room - call in advance to arrange. Packed lunches & meals not available on Saturday or Sunday. Call in advance to arrange horsebox parking

ARDINGTON

⊹ SU4388 🥾 2.5 miles (4km)

🚆 Didcot 6 miles (10km) 📞

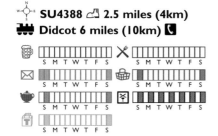

Pub: Boar's Head 01235 833254

FARNBOROUGH

⊹ SU4382 🥾 1.8 miles (2.9km)

🚆 Newbury 11.3 miles (18km)

The Old Smithy ↻

Mrs Lorna Gwinner

Farnborough, Wantage OX12 8NX

T: 01488 638782 **F:** 01488 638092

E: angus@wordsmith-ltd.com

🛏 1 £50 🛏 1 £50 (£35) 🚫 🖼 V

🥾 🚲 DRY 🔲 🚗 🐾

⚑ Stabling for horses can be arranged in advance with neighbour

WEST HENDRED

⊹ SU4488 🥾 2.5 miles (4km)

🚆 Didcot 6 miles (9km) 📞

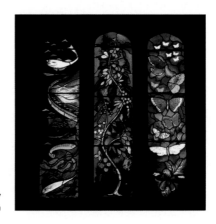

Pub: Hare 01235 833249

John Piper window in Farnborough church

EAST HENDRED

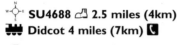 **SU4688** 🖍 **2.5 miles (4km)**
🚂 **Didcot 4 miles (7km)** 📞

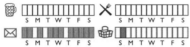

☆ Champs Chapel Museum - Open
Sundays only (limited opening Oct - Mar)
T: 01235 833312
www.hendred.org/champs.htm

☆ Hendred Vineyard
T: 01235 833277
http://home.freeuk.com/hendred/
busines03.htm

A Monk's Court

Ms Susan Turnbull
Newbury Road, East Hendred, Wantage
OX12 8LG
T: 01235 833797 **M:** 07710 274653
F: 01235 862554 **E:** udsl@udg.org.uk
www.monkscourt.co.uk
🛏 2 £55 🛏 1 £55 (£35) 🚭 ♿ ♿
📷 V 🏔 🚴 **DRY** 🔲 🚗 ◆◆◆ Some
rooms en-suite
🏕 3 £5 with field shelter
🐴 Call in advance to arrange horsebox
parking

Cowdrays   *closed Xmas & Easter*

Mrs Margaret Bateman
Cat Street, East Hendred, Wantage
OX12 8JT
T: 01235 833313 **M:** 07799 622003
E: cowdrays@virgin.net
🛏 2 £70 🛏 2 £60 (£30) 🛏 1 £30
🚭 ♿ ♿ 📷 V 🏔 🚴 **DRY** 🔲 🚗 🐴
◆◆◆

Greensands Guest House

Mr Leslie Wells
Reading Road, East Hendred, Wantage
OX12 8JE
T: 01235 833338 **M:** 07850 437013
F: 01235 821632
E: susannabowen@yahoo.co.uk
www.greensandsguesthouse.co.uk
🛏 4 £70 🛏 1 £70 🛏 1 £100 🛏 1
£35 🚭 ♿ ♿ 📷 V **DRY** 🔲 **VISA**
Mastercard, Visa. All rooms en-suite

WEST ILSLEY

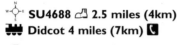 **SU4782** 🖍 **1.2 miles (2km)**
🚂 **Didcot 7 miles (11km)** 📞

Pub: Harrow Inn 01635 281260

CHILTON

SU4986 🥾 1.2 miles (2km)
🚂 Didcot 4 miles (6km) 📞

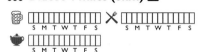

Pub: Rose & Crown 01235 862992

EAST ILSLEY

SU4981 🥾 1.2 miles (2km)
🚂 Didcot 7 miles (11km) 📞

Crown & Horns Inn

Mrs Sally Allsop
The Square, East Ilsley RG20 7LH
T: 01635 281545 F: 0870 1312567
E: crownandhorns@btinternet.com
🛏 6 £70 ⬦ 1 £70 ⬦ 3 £75 (£60)
🚫 ♟ 📷 V 🥾 ◐ 🚲 VISA
Mastercard, Visa, American Express,
Delta. All rooms en-suite
⬛ Laundry and drying facilities by
arrangement

UPTON

SU5186 🥾 2.5 miles (4km)
🚂 Didcot 3 miles (5km) 📞

Pub: George & Dragon 01235 850723

Prospect House O

Mrs Hilary Powell
Upton, Didcot OX11 9HU
T: 01235 850268 M: 07966 205688
E: srjpowell@lineone.net
🛏 2 £65 ⬦ 1 £65 (£35) 🚫 ♟ V
🚲 DRY ◐ ◆◆◆◆
🌙 2 £10

The White House
closed Xmas & New Year

Miss Heather Simper
Reading Road, Upton, Didcot
OX11 9HP
T: 01235 850289
⬦ 2 £50 (£28) 🚫 ♟ (min age 12) V
🥾 🚲 DRY 🚗 ◆◆◆◆

COMPTON

SU5280 🥾 1.2 miles (2km)
🚂 Goring 6 miles (9km) 📞

🖾 in store
Pub: Compton Swan Hotel 01635
578269

BLEWBURY

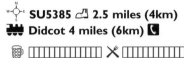 **SU5385** 2.5 miles (4km)
Didcot 4 miles (6km)

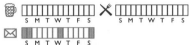

🏠 Red Lion

Mr Stuart Mace
Chapel Lane, Blewbury OX11 9PQ
T: 01235 850403 **F:** 01235 850666
E: enquiries@redlionblewbury.co.uk
www.redlionblewbury.co.uk
1 £50 1 £50 1 £60
Mastercard, Visa, American Express,
Delta. All rooms en-suite

Yew Tree

Mrs Liz Thacker
London Road, Blewbury OX11 9PF
T: 01235 850678 **F:** 01235 850678
E: lizthackeryewtree@hotmail.com
1 £40 (£55) 1 £35 (min
age 12) Some
rooms en-suite

ALDWORTH

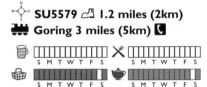 **SU5579** 1.2 miles (2km)
Goring 3 miles (5km)

Pubs: Bell 01635 578272 & Four Points
01635 578367

Fieldview Cottage   *closed Xmas*

Mr H Hunt
Bell Lane, Aldworth, Reading RG8 9SB
T: 01635 578964
E: hunt@fieldvu.freeserve.co.uk
1 £60 1 £60 (£30) 1 £30
♦♦♦♦

Aldworth church

The Four Points, Aldworth

MOULSFORD

 SU5983 🦶 1.2 miles (2km)
🚂 Cholsey 2 miles (3km) 📞

🍺 |||||||||||||| ✕ ||||||||||||||
    S M T W T F S   S M T W T F S
🧺 ||||||||||||||
    S M T W T F S

Pub: Beetle & Wedge 01491 651381

White House	closed Xmas & New Year

Mrs Maria Watsham
White House, Moulsford, Wallingford
OX10 9JD
T: 01491 651397 **M:** 07831 372243
F: 01491 652560
E: mwatsham@tiscali.co.uk
www.stayatwhitehouse.co.uk
🛏 1 £60 🛏 1 £60 (£40) 🛏 1 £40
🚭 👫 V 🐾 🚲 DRY 🗑 🚗 🏊
◆◆◆◆
🛏 Private bathroom available.
VisitBritain Silver Award

Beetle & Wedge Boathouse

Miss Stephanie Hicks
Ferry Lane, Moulsford OX10 9JF
T: 01491 651381 **F:** 01491 651376
E: stephaniehicks@hotmail.com
🛏 1 £90 (£75) 🚭 👫 V 🐾 🚲
DRY 🗑 VISA Mastercard, Visa, American
Express, Delta. Room is en-suite
🛏 Double room can be a twin room if
required

STREATLEY

✛ **SU5980** 👢 **on path**
🚂 **Goring & Streatley 0.5 miles (1km)** 📞

🍺 ▯▯▯▯▯▯▯▯▯▯▯ ✕ ▯▯▯▯▯▯▯▯▯▯▯
   S M T W T F S   S M T W T F S

Pubs: Swan at Streatley 01491 878800 & Bull 01491 872392

☆ The Holies Nature Reserve
T: 0118 984 3040
www.nationaltrust.org.uk

☆ Basildon Park
T: 01494 755558
www.nationaltrust.org.uk

☆ Beale Wildlife Park
T: 0118 9845172
www.bealepark.co.uk

[INN] The Bull at Streatley

Mrs A J Booker
Reading Road, Streatley RG8 9JJ
T: 01491 872392 **F:** 01491 875231
E: bull@inntownpub.com
www.thebullatstreatley.com
🛏 6 £70 (£70) 🚫 ♯♀ 📷 V 🐾 🌀
🚲 💳 Mastercard, Visa, American Express, Delta ◆◆◆ All rooms en-suite

The Swan at Streatley 🏠

Mr Karl Bentley
Streatley RG8 9HR
T: 01491 878800 **F:** 01491 872554
E: sales@swan-at-streatley.co.uk
www.swanatstreatley.co.uk
🛏 27 £105 🛏 9 £105 🛏 3 £135 (£90) 🛏 8 £80 ♯♀ ♿ 📷 V 🐾 🌀 🗑 📷
💳 Mastercard, Visa, American Express, Delta ★★★★ All rooms en-suite

YHA Streatley *closed Nov-Feb* ▲S

Mr Nick Crivich
Hill House, Reading Road, Streatley RG8 9JJ
T: 01491 872278 **F:** 01491 873056
E: streatley@yha.org.uk
www.yhastreatley.org.uk
🛏 2 £40 🛏 8 £56 (£30) 🚫 ♯♀ V 🐾 🌀 🚲 DRY 💳 Mastercard, Visa, Delta ★★★ Some rooms en-suite
🅷 Dormitory/private accommodation available. Self-catering accommodation from £15.50 per unit

Crab apple

3 Ickneild Cottages

Mrs Susan Brodie
3 Ickneild Cottages, High Street,
Streatley RG8 9JA
T: 01491 875152 **F:** 01491 875650
🛏 I £25 🚭 **V** ☂ 🚲 **DRY** 🅿 🚗 🚶

Stable Cottages ○

Mrs Diana Fenton
Wallingford Road, Streatley RG8 9JX
T: 01491 874408
🛏 I £50 (£25) 🛏 I £25 🚭 👪 (min age 8) **V** ☂ 🚲 **DRY** 🅿 🚶
Ⓢ 2 £10

Lock at Goring-on-Thames

Grim's Ditch

St Botolph's, Swyncombe, early Norman church dedicated to the patron saint of travellers

Section

Streatley to Watlington

At the start of this 15.3 miles (24.6km) section The Ridgeway crosses another National Trail, the Thames Path, before following the bank of the River Thames for a few picturesque miles. The Trail then heads east into the more wooded Chilterns via an ancient Grim's Ditch and finishes on the wide track of the old Icknield Way.

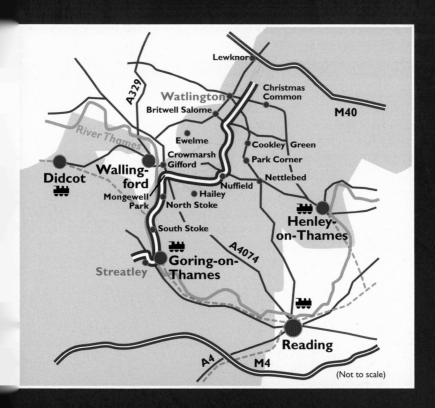

(Not to scale)

Maps

Landranger maps	174	Newbery and Wantage
	175	Reading and Windsor
Explorer maps	171	Chiltern Hills West

Taxis

Place	Name	Telephone Number
Aston Upthorpe	Astons Airport Services	07837 343680
Goring-on-Thames	Murdocks Taxis	01491 872029
Wallingford	Hills Taxis	01491 837022
Nettlebed	David Byers of Nettlebed	01491 641159
Ewelme	Busher's Taxis	01491 826161

Car Parking

If you choose to park in villages close to The Ridgeway, please park considerately. Other places to park are listed below but you need to be aware that theft from cars parked in the countryside does occur. You are advised to leave any unnecessary items at home or, failing that, ensure that anything valuable is locked in the boot of your vehicle.

Place	Map Grid Reference
Goring-on-Thames public car park	SU 599807
On Ridgeway on west side of minor road, 1 mile (1 1/2km) from Britwell Salome heading southeast	SU 681922
On Ridgeway on east side of Hill Road, minor road to Christmas Common 1/2 mile (1km) southeast of Watlington	SU 698940

Water Points

Place	Map Grid Reference
Grimsdyke Cottage, Grim's Ditch	SU 660872
Church, Nuffield (on the wall)	SU 667874
White Mark Farm Camp Site, Watlington (March - October)	SU 697939

Toilets

Place	Map Grid Reference
Goring-on-Thames (Car Park off Station Road)	SU 602807
White Mark Farm Camp Site, Watlington (March - October)	SU 697939
Watlington (High Street)	SU 689945

Vets

Place	Name	Telephone Number
Goring-on-Thames	The Goring Veterinary Centre	01491 873638
Wallingford	White TD & Stewart JD	01491 839043
Watlington	Larkmead Vets Domestic Pets	01491 612799

Farriers

Place	Name	Telephone Number
Watlington	William Smith	01491 612872
	Adrian Spilsbury	01491 613399

Saddlers

Place	Name	Telephone Number
Blewbury	Arena Saddlery	01235 850725

Bike Repairs

Place	Name	Telephone Number
Pangbourne	Mountain High	0118 984 1851
Wallingford	Rides on Air	01491 836289

Mountain Bike Hire

Place	Name	Telephone Number
Abingdon	Pedal Power	01235 525123
Pangbourne	Mountain High	0118 984 1851

Tourist Information Centres

This TIC is staffed but note that many libraries in the area have leaflets about local attractions and events.

Place	Address/Opening Hours
Wallingford	Wallingford One Stop Shop, Town Hall, Market Place, Wallingford OX10 0EG **T**: 01491 826972 **F**: 01491 832925 **W**: www.sodc.com Opening hours: Call in advance to check

Brunel's railway bridge over the Thames between South and North Stoke

GORING-ON-THAMES

SU6080 on path
Goring & Streatley 📞 🚻
♿WC

🍺	S M T W T F S	✕	S M T W T F S
✉	S M T W T F S	🧺	S M T W T F S
🫖	S M T W T F S	✂	S M T W T F S
	S W T F S		

£ HSBC, Lloyds TSB

Melrose Cottage

Mrs Rosemary Howarth
36 Milldown Road, Goring-on-Thames
RG8 0BD
T: 01491 873040 M: 07798 663897
2 £50 (£30) 1 £30 V

Northview House *closed Xmas*

Mrs I Sheppard
Farm Road, Goring-on-Thames RG8
0AA
T: 01491 872184 E: hi@goring-on-thames.freeserve.co.uk
2 £50 1 £50 1 £65 (£30)

🏨 The Queens Arms

Mrs L McAuliffe
Reading Road, Goring-on-Thames
RG8 0ER
T: 01491 872825 M: 07834 767233
E: queensarms_goring@fsmail.net
1 £60 1 £60 (£35) 2 £30
(min age 10) V

SOUTH STOKE

SU5983 on path
Goring & Streatley 2 miles
(3km) 📞

| 🍺 | S M T W T F S | ✕ | S M T W T F S |

Pub: Perch & Pike 01491 872415

The Oak Barn

Mrs Vanessa Guiver
The Old Post Office, South Stoke,
Reading RG8 0JS
T: 01491 871872 M: 07889 757767
F: 01491 871873 E: info@oakbarn.org
www.oakbarn.org
1 £70
Room is en-suite

South Stoke church

71

NORTH STOKE

SU6086 on path
Goring & Streatley 4 miles (6km)

S M T W T F S   S M T W T F S

Pub: Springs Hotel 01491 836687

The Springs Hotel & Golf Club

Mr George Briffa
Wallingford Road, North Stoke,
Wallingford OX10 6BE
T: 01491 836687
E: info@thespringshotel.com
www.thespringshotel.com
19 £105 10 £105 3 £135
(£95) Mastercard, Visa, American Express.
All rooms en-suite

CROWMARSH GIFFORD

SU6189 0.6 miles (1km)
Didcot 6 miles (10km)

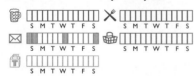
S M T W T F S   S M T W T F S
S M T W T F S   S M T W T F S
S M T W T F S

Pubs: Queen's Head 01491 839857 &
Bell Inn (Hungry Horse) 01491 835324

Little Gables

Mr & Mrs Tony & Jill Reeves
166 Crowmarsh Hill, Wallingford
OX10 8BG
T: 01491 837834 **M:** 07860 148882
F: 01491 834426
E: jill@stayingaway.com
www.stayingaway.com
2 £55 2 £55 (£45) 2 £75
1 £45 Some rooms en-suite
◆◆◆◆ Some rooms en-suite

Bridge Villa Camping & Caravan Park   *closed Jan*

Mr A Townsend
The Street, Crowmarsh Gifford,
Wallingford OX10 8HB
T: 01491 836860 **M:** 07710 452429
F: 01491 836793
E: bridge.villa@btinternet.com
Numerous £8 Numerous £11
WC CG Mastercard, Visa, Delta
Quality standard rating applied for.
111 pitches in total

Riverside Park   *closed Oct-mid April*

Mr Jeremy Mayo
The Street, Wallingford Bridge,
Crowmarsh Gifford, Wallingford
OX10 8EB
T: 01491 835232
www.soll-leisure.co.uk
15 £10 9 £10 WC
24 pitches in total

WALLINGFORD

 **SU6089** ◱ 1.2 miles (2km)
🚅 **Cholsey 6 miles (9km)** 🛈

Market town with full range of services, visit www.wallingfordtown.co.uk for further details. It has a wide range of accommodation and details can be obtained from the Tourist Information point - details in the introduction section.

☆ Wallingford Museum
T: 01491 835065
www.galatham.demon.co.uk

☆ Wallingford Castle
www.berkshirehistory.com/castles/wallingford_cast.html

🕀 The George Hotel

Mr Oliver Round-Turner
High Street, Wallingford OX10 0BS
T: 01491 836665 F: 01491 825359
E: info@george-hotel-wallingford.com
www.peelhotel.com
🛏 9 £95 ⚏ 20 £95 ⚏ 1 £105
(£80) ⚏ 9 £60 ⚤ ♿ V 🏃 🛇 🚲
DRY VISA Mastercard, Visa, American Express, Switch ★★★ All rooms en-suite
🚬 Smoking permitted in some rooms

52 Blackstone Road

Mrs Enid Barnard
Wallingford OX10 8JL
T: 01491 839339
E: enid.barnard@mediummail.co.uk
🛏 1 £35 (£23) ⚏ 1 £18 🚭 V 🏃
🚲 DRY

The Studio

Mrs Pamela Mary Smith
85 Wantage Road, Wallingford
OX10 0LT
T: 01491 837277 F: 01491 825036
E: pam@prufit.co.uk
www.prufit.co.uk
🛏 1 £50 ⚏ 1 £50 (£35) ⚏ 1 £25
🚭 ⚤ (min age 3) 🂫 V 🏃 🚲 DRY 🍴
🚶 All rooms en-suite

HAILEY

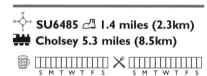 **SU6485** ◱ 1.4 miles (2.3km)
🚅 **Cholsey 5.3 miles (8.5km)**

🍺 |||||||||||| ✕ ||||||||||||
  S M T W T F S   S M T W T F S
Pub: King William IV 01491 681845

Spindle

NUFFIELD

☖ **SU6687** ⛺ **on path**
🚉 **Henley-on-Thames 7 miles (11km)** 📞

🍺 |S M T W T F S| ✕ |S M T W T F S|

Pub: Crown Inn 01491 641335

☆ Nuffield Place
T: 01491 641224
www.nuffield-place.com

Mays Farm

⛢ GR SU654885 1.3 miles (2.1km) from Ridgeway
Mrs P Passmore
Ewelme, Wallingford OX10 6QF
T: 01491 641294 F: 01491 641191
🛏 1 £50 🛏 1 £52 (£34) 🛏 1 £27
🚭 ⛄ V 🛋 DRY 🚗 ◆◆◆◆ Some rooms en-suite

14 Bradley Road *closed Xmas & New Year*

Miss Diana Chambers
Nuffield, Henley-on-Thames RG9 5SG
T: 01491 641359 M: 07946 909771
F: 01491 641359
E: diana.chambers@tiscali.co.uk
🛏 2 £54 🛏 1 £54 (£30) 🚭 ⛄ 🐾
V 🛋 🚲 DRY 🔘 🚶 Some rooms en-suite

The Rectory ⛺

Mr John Shearer
Nuffield, Henley-on-Thames RG9 5SN
T: 01491 641305 F: 01491 641305
🛏 1 £40 🛏 1 £40 (£30) 🛏 1 £20
🚭 ⛄ V 🛋 🚲 DRY 🔘 🚶
⛺ 5 £2/person 🚐 1 £5 🔥 🔥 ♿
🚲 DRY 🔘

NETTLEBED

☖ **SU70787** ⛺ **2.9 miles (4.6km)**
🚉 **Henley-on-Thames 5.2 miles (8.4km)**

🍺 |S M T W T F S| ✕ |S M T W T F S|
✉ |S M T W T F S| 🧺 |S M T W T F S|
🫖 |S M T W T F S|

Pub: White Hart Hotel 01491 641245

White Hart Hotel 🅗

Mr J C Roumignac
High Street, Nettlebed, Henley-on-Thames RG9 5DD
T: 01491 641245 F: 01491 649018
E: info@whitehartnettlebed.com
www.whitehartnettlebed.com
🛏 8 £60 🛏 1 £60 🛏 3 £60 (£60)
🚭 ⛄ ♿ 🐾 V 🛋 🌀 🚲 DRY 🔘 🚶
💳 Mastercard, Visa, American Express, Switch/Maestro ★★★ All rooms en-suite
🅜 Has one Michelin star

Somerset

Mrs Nan McDonnell
9 High Street, Nettlebed, Henley-on-
Thames RG9 5DA
T: 01491 641710
E: jobs@mcdonnell14.freeserve.co.uk
🚲 2 £52 (£26) 🚭 ❄ (min age 6) **V**
🚲 **DRY** 🚗 👣 All rooms en-suite

EWELME

SU6491 🥾 1.3 miles (2.1km)
🚌 Henley-on-Thames 10.6 miles
(17km) 📞

🍺 |||||||||| ✕ ||||||||||
 S M T W T F S   S M T W T F S
Pub: Shepherd's Hut 01491 835661

Fords Farm

Miss M Edwards
Ewelme, Wallingford OX10 6HU
T: 01491 839272
E: fordsfarm@callnetuk.com
www.fordsfarm.co.uk
🛏 1 £60 🚲 2 £60 (£40) 🚭 **V** 🧖
🚲 **DRY** 🚗 👣 ◆◆◆◆ Some
rooms en-suite
🏅 VisitBritain Silver Award.

PARK CORNER

SU6988 🥾 1.2 miles (2km)
🚌 Henley-on-Thames 6 miles
(10km)

Park Corner Farmhouse ○

Mrs S M Rutter
Park Corner, Nettlebed, Henley-on-
Thames RG9 6DX
T: 01491 641450
E: parkcorner_farmhouse@hotmail.com
🚲 2 £55 (£30) 🛏 1 £30 🚭 ❄ 📺
V 🧖 🚲 🚗 👣 ◆◆◆
(S) 2 £10 🍳 4 £6

COOKLEY GREEN

SU6990 🥾 0.8 miles (1.2km)
🚌 Henley-on-Thames 7.5 miles
(12km) 📞

Pathways   *closed Xmas*

Mrs Ismayne Peters
Cookley Green, Swyncombe, Henley-
on-Thames RG9 6EN
T: 01491 641631
E: ismayne.peters@tesco.net
🛏 1 £55 🚲 2 £55 (£35) 🚭 ❄
(min age 12) 🛆 **V** 🧖 🕭 🚲 **DRY** 📷
🚗 👣 All rooms en-suite

BRITWELL SALOME

SU6787 🥾 0.6 miles (1km)
🚌 Henley-on-Thames 11 miles
(17km) 📞

🍺 |||||||||| ✕ ||||||||||
 S M T W T F S   S M T W T F S
Pub: Goose 01491 612304

WATLINGTON

 **SU6894** 🏠 **0.6 miles (1km)**
🚂 **Henley-on-Thames 10 miles (16km)** 📞 ♿

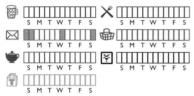

£ Barclays, 🏧 in Co-Op
☆ Watlington Hill and White Mark
www.nationaltrust.org.uk

A Woodgate Orchard Cottage

Ms Ronnie Roberts
Howe Road, Watlington OX49 5EL
T: 01491 612675
E: mailbox@wochr.freeserve.co.uk
🛏 2 £50 🛏 2 £50 (£35) 🛏 2 £35
🚫 ⚦ 📺 V 🅰 🌳 🚲 DRY 🔘 🚗 🐾
◆◆◆ Some rooms en-suite
🅷 Organic food available. Evening meal
by prior arrangement

White Mark Farm *closed 31 Oct - 1 Mar*

Mrs Rosemary Williams
82 Hill Road, Watlington OX49 5AF
T: 01491 612295
🅰 Numerous £4/person 🚐 5
£4/person 🚻 🚰 🚰 ♿ 🚿 🚲 DRY

Looking from Ladies walk to Jacob's tent, Swyncombe

Section 5

Watlington to Wendover

This 17 miles (27.2km) stretch is probably the most strenuous part of The Ridgeway. It starts out gently enough following the wide track of the Icknield Way but once it departs from this it climbs in and out of several Chilterns valleys. Passing through some lovely nature reserves the Trail reaches a high point with fantastic views at Coombe Hill before descending to Wendover. If you haven't already seen a red kite, you're guaranteed to see one on this stretch!

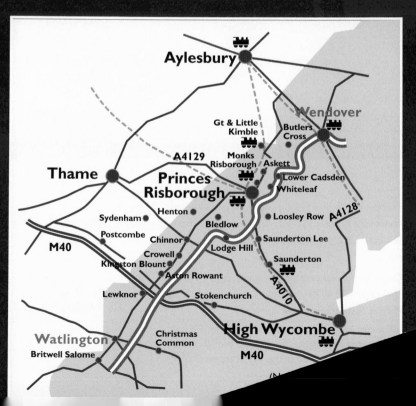

Maps

Landranger maps	175	Reading and Windsor
	165	Aylesbury and Leighton Buzzard
Explorer maps	171	Chiltern Hills West
	181	Chiltern Hills North

Taxis

Place	Name	Telephone Number
Ewelme	Busher's Taxis	01491 826161
Chinnor	Chinnor Cabs	01844 353637
	D & J Cabs	01844 353344
Loosley Row	Springline Cars	01844 274474
Princes Risborough	Risborough Cars	01844 274111
	Village Cars	01844 342551
	B&V Taxis	01844 342079
	Red Line Cars	01844 343736
Butlers Cross	Chilton Taxis	07721 677687
Wendover	Alexander's at Wendover	01296 620888

Car Parking

If you choose to park in villages close to The Ridgeway, please park considerately. Other places to park are listed below but you need to be aware that theft from cars parked in the countryside does occur. You are advised to leave any ...essary items at home or, failing that, ensure that anything valuable is locked in ...f your vehicle.

	Map Grid Reference
...t side of minor road to Bledlow Ridge	
...hinnor	SP 761003
...park	SP 810034
...east of Princes	
...nks Risborough	
...	SP 824036

(Not to scale)

Place	Map Grid Reference
National Trust car park for Coombe Hill, 1 mile (2km) southwest of Wendover. From Wendover travel west on minor road to Princes Risborough. Take first left, then first left again. At top of hill car park is on left	SP 852062
Wendover public car park	SP 868077

Water Points

Place	Map Grid Reference
White Mark Farm Camp Site, Watlington (March - October)	SU 697939

Toilets

Place	Map Grid Reference
Watlington (High Street)	SU 689945
White Mark Farm Camp Site, Watlington (March- October)	SU 697939
Princes Risborough (Horn Mill Car Park)	SP 809033
Wendover (Library Car Park)	SP 868078

Vets

Place	Name	Telephone Number
Watlington	Larkmead Vets Domestic Pets	01491 612799
Stokenchurch	Hall Place Veterinary Centre	01494 485855
Princes Risborough	Sprinz & Nash	01844 345655
Halton	Wendover Heights Veterinary Centre	01296 623439

Farriers

Place	Name	Telephone Number
Watlington	William Smith	01491 612872
	Adrian Spilsbury	01491 613399
Chinnor	Malcolm Woodward	01844 354427
Stokenchurch	John Jennings	01494 485003
	David Matthews	01494 484413
	Jonathan Smith	07717 292445

Bike Repairs

Place	Name	Telephone Number
Thame	Thame Cycles	01844 261520
Princes Risborough	Boltons Bikes	01844 345949

Mountain Bike Hire

Place	Name	Telephone Number
Princes Risborough	Boltons Bikes	01844 345949

Tourist Information Centres

These TICs are staffed but note that many libraries in the area have leaflets about local attractions and events.

★ offers accommodation booking service (until 15:30)

Place	Address/Opening Hours
Wallingford	Wallingford One Stop Shop, Town Hall, Market Place, Wallingford OX10 0EG T: 01491 826972 F: 01491 832925 W: www.sodc.com Opening hours: Call in advance to check
Princes Risborough	Tower Court, Horns Lane, Princes Risborough HP27 0AJ T: 01844 274795 F: 01844 275795 W: www.princesrisborough.com Opening hours: All year: Mon-Fri 09:00-17:00
★ Wendover	The Clock Tower, High Street, Wendover HP22 6DU T: 01296 696759 F: 0871 2361551 E: tourism@wendover-pc.gov.uk W: www.chilternweb.co.uk/wendover Opening hours: All year: Mon-Sat 10:00-16:00

CHRISTMAS COMMON

SU7193 🥾 **1.3 miles (2.1km)**
🚂 **Henley-on-Thames 9.6 miles
(15.4km)** 📞

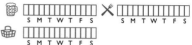
S M T W T F S   S M T W T F S

Pub: Fox & Hounds 01491 612599

LEWKNOR

SU7197 🥾 **0.6 miles (1km)**
🚂 **Princes Risborough 7 miles
(12km)** 📞

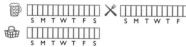
S M T W T F S   S M T W T F S
S M T W T F S

Pub: Leathern Bottle 01844 351482

☆ Chiltern Sculpture Trail
T: 01865 778918
www.chilternsculpturetrail.co.uk

Moorcourt Cottage

Mrs Eppy Hodgson
Weston Road, Lewknor OX49 5RU
T: 01844 351419
🛏 1 £50 🛏 1 £50 (£35) 🚭 🕴 V
🚲 DRY 🔲 🚗 🚶 ◆◆◆◆
🅷 Family room can be arranged in
advance

POSTCOMBE

SU7099 🥾 **1.6 miles (2.5km)**
🚂 **Princes Risborough 8 miles
(13km)** 📞

S M T W T F S   S M T W T F S
S M T W T F S

Pub: England's Rose 01844 281383

Beech Farm

Mrs Jackie Graham
Salt Lane, Postcombe, Thame OX9 7EE
T: 01844 281240 **M:** 07973 506443
E: beech.farm@btopenworld.com
www.beechfarm.co.uk
🛏 2 £50 (£35) 🛏 1 £35 🚭 🕴 (min
age 7 years) ♿ 🔲 V 🏍 🚲 DRY 🔲
🚗 🚶 ◆◆◆◆ All rooms en-suite

**Aston Rowant
National Nature Reserve**

ASTON ROWANT

⊕ **SU7298** 🔲 **0.6 miles (1km)**
🚆 **Princes Risborough 6 miles (10km)** 📞

S M T W T F S   S M T W T F S

Pub: Lambert Arms 01844 351496

☆ Aston Rowant National Nature Reserve
T: 01844 351833
www.english-nature.org.uk

Tower Cottage

Mrs Margaret Mason
Chinnor Road, Aston Rowant
OX49 5SH
T: 01844 354676 M: 07721 676150
F: 01844 355999
E: towercottagebb@aol.com
www.tower-cottage.co.uk
🛏 1 £50 🛏 2 £45 🛏 1 £65 (£35) 🚭 ✻ (min age 7) 🔲 V 🔥 🚲 DRY 🔲
🚶 ◆◆◆ Some rooms en-suite

🏨 The Lambert Arms

Mr Roger Romyn
London Road, Aston Rowant OX49 5SB
T: 01844 353496 F: 01844 351893
E: info@lambertarms.co.uk
www.lambertarms.co.uk
🛏 7 £70 (£65) 🛏 1 £115 🛏 1 £50
🚭 ✻ ♿ 🔲 V 🔥 🕭 🚲 DRY 💳
Mastercard, Visa, Delta. All rooms en-suite

STOKENCHURCH

⊕ **SU7696** 🔲 **2.7 miles (4.3km)**
🚆 **Princes Risborough or High Wycombe 7.3 miles (11.7km)** 📞

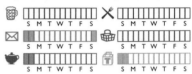
S M T W T F S   S M T W T F S
S M T W T F S   S M T W T F S
S M T W T F S   S M T W T F S

£ Lloyds TSB & two 🏧 in local stores

Hallbottom Farm   U

Mrs Deborah Abbot
Park Lane, Stokenchurch HP14 3TQ
T: 01494 482520 M: 07778 216024
E: deborah@hallbottomfarm.co.uk
www.hallbottomfarm.co.uk
🛏 4 £60 🛏 2 £60 (£40) 🚭 ✻
(min age 8) V 🚲 DRY ◆◆◆◆ Some rooms en-suite
🔖 4 £20

KINGSTON BLOUNT

⊕ **SU7399** 🔲 **0.5 miles (0.8km)**
🚆 **Princes Risborough 6 miles (10km)** 📞

S M T W T F S   S M T W T F S

Pub: Cherry Tree 01844 352273

A Lakeside Town Farm

Mrs Clark
Town Farm Cottage, Brook Street,
Kingston Blount OX39 4RZ
T: 01844 352152 **M:** 07971 436504
F: 01844 352152
E: townfarmcottage@oxfree.com
www.townfarmcottage.co.uk
🛏 I £70 🛏 I £70 🛏 I £70 (£45)
🚭 ♀♂ (min age 10) **V** 🚲 **DRY** VISA
Mastercard, Visa, Delta ◆◆◆◆ All
rooms en-suite
▉ Two nights minimum stay

The Chilterns

Area of Outstanding Natural Beauty

Caring for the Chilterns

You can help the Chilterns by

*   Enjoying, understanding and
    caring for the chilterns

*   Leaving your car at home

*   Showing respect to other users of
    the countryside

*   Supporting the local economy -
    buy local products and services

*   Not disrupting the activities of
    those who make their living from
    the countryside

*   Taking pride in the Chilterns -
    follow the Country Code

CROWELL

⊹ **SU7499** 🏠 **0.5 miles (0.8km)**
🚂 **Princes Risborough 5.6 miles
(9km)**

🍺 |||||||||||||| ✕ ||||||||||||||
    S M T W T F S   S M T W T F S

Pub: Shepherd's Crook 01844 351431

CHINNOR

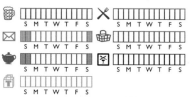

⊹ **SP7500** 🏠 **0.6 miles (1km)**
🚂 **Princes Risborough 4 miles
(7km)** 📞 ♿ ♿WC

🍺 |||||||||||||| ✕ ||||||||||||||
    S M T W T F S   S M T W T F S
✉ |||||||||||||| 🧺 ||||||||||||||
    S M T W T F S   S M T W T F S
🫖 |||||||||||||| 🈯 ||||||||||||||
    S M T W T F S   S M T W T F S
💊 ||||||||||||||
    S M T W T F S

£ Royal Bank of Scotland, 🏧 in Co-op

☆ Chinnor Hill Nature Reserve
T: 01865 775476 www.bbowt.org.uk

☆ Chinnor and Princes Risborough
Railway
T: 01844 353535
http://www.cprra.co.uk/

Station Road Bed & Breakfast

Mr Peter Snow
7 Station Road, Chinnor OX39 4PU
T: 01844 351889 **F:** 01844 351889
E: peter@snow.fsnet.co.uk
🛏 2 £45 (£30) I £30 🚭 ♀♂ 🖐 **V**
🥾 🚲 **DRY** 🔲 🛝

HENTON

⌖ SP7602 🥾 1 miles (1.5km)
🚆 Princes Risborough 3 miles (5km) 📞

Pub: Peacock 01844 353519

Manor Farm Cottage

Mr & Mrs Trevor & Jean Dixon
Henton, Chinnor OX39 4AE
T: 01844 353301 M: 07889 441601
E: dixonhenton@aol.com
www.manorfarmcottage.info
🛏 1 £55 🛏 1 £55 (£38) 🚭 ⋔ 📷
V 🚶 🚲 DRY ⊚ 🧍 ◆◆◆

BLEDLOW

⌖ SP7702 🥾 0.6 miles (1km)
🚆 Princes Risborough 2 miles (3km) 📞

Pub: Lions of Bledlow 01844 343345

LODGE HILL

⌖ SP7900 🥾 on path
🚆 Princes Risborough 2 miles (3km)

Old Callow Down Farm

⌖ GR SU787000 100m from Ridgeway
Mr & Mrs C J Gee
Wigans Lane, Bledlow Ridge, High
Wycombe HP14 4BH
T: 01844 344416 F: 01844 344703
E: oldcallow@aol.com
www.chilternscottage.co.uk
🛏 1 £50 (£35) 🚭 ⋔占 📷 V 🚶
🚲 DRY ⊚ 🧍 Room is en-suite

SAUNDERTON LEE

⌖ SP7901 🥾 0.6 miles (1km)
🚆 Saunderton 1.2 miles (2km)

Pub: Rose & Crown 01844 345299

LOOSLEY ROW

⌖ SP8100 🥾 1.1 miles (1.7km)
🚆 Saunderton 2.4 miles (3.8km)

The Greenhills Garden Apartment   SC

Mrs D O Dean
Greenhills, Little Lane, Loosley Row,
Princes Risborough HP27 0NX
T: 01844 342409 M: 07940 211079
E: dormic@aol.com
🛏 1 £70 🛏 2 £90 (£55) 🚭 ⋔
🚲 DRY 🧍 VISA Mastercard, Visa,
American Express, Delta. All rooms en-suite

🏠 Self-catering accommodation also available from £70/night for 2 sharing

PRINCES RISBOROUGH

⊕ **SP8003** 👢 **on path**
🚃 **Princes Risborough 🅸**

Market town with full range of services, visit www.visitbuckinghamshire.org for further details.

☆ Princes Risborough Manor House
T: 01494 755573
www.nationaltrust.org.uk

Coppins B&B

Mrs Jill Thomas
New Road, Princes Risborough
HP27 0LA
T: 01844 344508 M: 07745 596103
E: jillthomas@thecoppins.co.uk
www.thecoppins.co.uk
🛏 2 £48 (£33) 🚭 ⚤ (min age 5) V
🚴 🚲 DRY ⬚ 🚶 ◆◆◆◆
🅷 Twin rooms can be made into double rooms

WHITELEAF

⊕ **SP8204** 👢 **0.6 miles (1km)**
🚃 **Monks Risborough 1 miles
(1.5km)**

🍺 |||||||||||| ✗ ||||||||||||
S M T W T F S   S M T W T F S
Pub: Red Lion 01844 344476

☆ Whiteleaf Hill and Cross
www.buckscc.gov.uk/countryside/whiteleaf

LOWER CADSDEN

⊕ **SP8204** 👢 **on path**
🚃 **Monks Risborough 1 miles
(2km)**

🍺
S M T W T F S   S M T W T F S
Pub: Plough at Cadsden 01844 343302

☆ Grangelands and Pulpit Hill Nature Reserve www.nationaltrust.org.uk

ASKETT

⊕ **SP8105** 👢 **1.2 miles (2km)**
🚃 **Monks Risborough 0.5 miles
(1km) 🅲**

🍺
S M T W T F S   S M T W T F S
Pubs: Three Crowns 01844 343041 &
Black Horse 01844 345296

Solis Ortu

Mrs Pamela Crockett
Aylesbury Road, Askett, Princes
Risborough HP27 9LY
T: 01844 347777 F: 01844 343509
E: pamela@crockettandson.co.uk
🛏 1 £50 🚭 1 £50 (£25) 🚭 ⚤
(min age 10) V 🚴 🚲 🚗 ◆◆◆
🅷 Private bathroom available

GREAT KIMBLE

⊕ **SU8206** 0.6 miles (1km)
🚆 **Little Kimble 0.5 miles (1km)**
☎

🍺 |||||||||| ✕ ||||||||||
S M T W T F S   S M T W T F S
Pubs: Swan 01844 275288 & Bernard
Arms 01844 346172

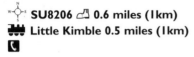

The Swan at Great Kimble

Mr Tim Woolnough
Grove Lane, Great Kimble, Aylesbury
HP17 9TR
T: 01844 275288
E: theswangtkimble@aol.com
🛏 | £70 2 £60 | £100
(£40) ♥♥ V 🔥 🍺 Mastercard,
Visa, Delta. All rooms en-suite

BUTLERS CROSS

⊕ **SP8407** 0.6 miles (1km)
🚆 **Little Kimble 1 miles (2km)** ☎
🍺 |||||||||| ✕ ||||||||||
S M T W T F S   S M T W T F S
Pub: Russell Arms 01296 622618

WENDOVER

⊕ **SP8607** on path
🚆 **Wendover** 🛈

Market town with full range of services,
visit www.visitbuckinghamshire.org for
further details. It has a good range of

accommodation and details can be
obtained from the Tourist Information
Centre - details in the introduction
section.

☆ Wendover Woods
T: 01420 520212
www.forestry.gov.uk

Belton House   *closed Dec 20-30* SC

Mrs E C Condie
26 Chiltern Road, Wendover HP22 6DB
T: 01296 622351
| £40 | £20/adult & £10/child
(£20) | £20 🚭 ♥♥ V 🔥 🚲
🍺 ◆
🍴 Self-catering option available at
£20/unit - food provided for breakfast

Dunsmore Edge   *closed Xmas & New Year*

Mr & Mrs Ron & Ursula Drackford
Dunsmore Lane, London Road,
Wendover HP22 6PN
T: 01296 623080 **E:** uron@lineone.net
🛏 | £52 | £55 (£30) | £30
🚭 ♥♥ (min age 5) ♿ V 🔥 🚲 🍺
◆◆◆ Some rooms en-suite

Mrs MacDonald's *closed Xmas & New Year*

Mrs Yvonne MacDonald
25 Witchell, Wendover HP22 6EG
T: 01296 623426
| £60 (£35) | £30 🚭 V 🔥
🚲 🍺 ◆◆◆
🍴 Private bathroom available

Section 6

Wendover to Ivinghoe Beacon

This 11.8 miles (18.8km) section is the most wooded of
The Ridgeway with extensive woods, many of beech, much of the
way. However once the Trail reaches Pitstone Hill the final few miles
are in open downland countryside reminiscent of the landscape
surrounding earlier stages. As a final flourish The Ridgeway finishes
on top of yet another Iron Age fort at Ivinghoe Beacon.

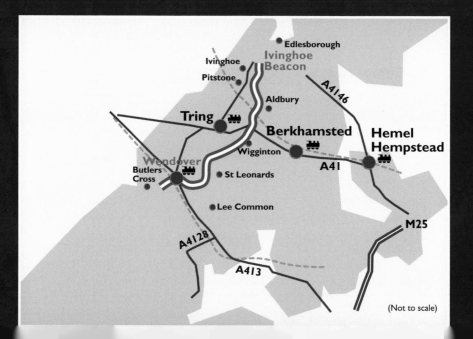

Maps

Landranger maps	165	Aylesbury and Leighton Buzzard
Explorer maps	181	Chiltern Hills North

Taxis

Place	Name	Telephone Number
Wendover	Alexander's at Wendover	01296 620888
Wigginton	T C Cabs	01442 875757
Wigginton	Diamond Cars	01442 890303
Tring	John Taxi's	01442 828828
	AAA Line Taxis	01442 890288
	Mike's Private Hire	01442 826161
	Airport Taxis of Tring	01442 828848
	Bev's Cars	01442 824105
	Aky Cars of Tring	01442 891234

Car Parking

If you choose to park in villages close to The Ridgeway, please park considerately. Other places to park are listed below but you need to be aware that theft from cars parked in the countryside does occur. You are advised to leave any unnecessary items at home or, failing that, ensure that anything valuable is locked in the boot of your vehicle.

Place	Map Grid Reference
Wendover public car park	SP 868077
Pitstone Hill car park east of Tring. From sharp bend on B488, 1/2 mile (1km) southeast of Ivinghoe, take minor road signposted Aldbury. Car park is on right after 1/2 mile (1km)	SP 955149
National Trust car park for Ivinghoe Beacon, on the left of minor road to Ringshall, 1/2 mile (1km) south off the B489	SP 962162

Toilets

Place	Map Grid Reference
Wendover (Library Car Park)	SP 868078

Vets

Place	Name	Telephone Number
Halton	Wendover Heights Veterinary Centre	01296 623439
Tring	Springwell Veterinary Surgery	01442 822151

Tourist Information Centres

These TICs are staffed but note that many libraries in the area have leaflets about local attractions and events.

★ offers accommodation booking service (until 15:30)

Place	Address/Opening Hours
★Wendover	The Clock Tower, High Street, Wendover HP22 6DU **T**: 01296 696759 **F**: 0871 2361551 **E**: tourism@wendover-pc.gov.uk **W**: www.chilternweb.co.uk/wendover Opening hours: All year: Mon-Sat 10:00-16:00
Tring	99 Akeman Street, Tring HP23 6AA **T**: 01442 823347 **F**: 01442 827178 **E**: info@tring.gov.uk **W**: www.tring.gov.uk Opening hours: All year: Mon-Sat 09:30-15:00, Sat 10:00-13:00

LEE COMMON

SP9004 1.9 miles (3km)
Wendover 4.5 miles (7.3km)
C

SC **Lower Bassibones Farm**
Mrs Anthea Hartley
Lee Common, Great Missenden
HP16 9LA
T: 01494 837798 **F:** 01494 837778
E: lowerbassibones@yahoo.co.uk
http://discover-real-england.com
2 £65 (£58) ✝✝ (min age 12) V
DRY Mastercard, Visa,
Delta ◆◆◆◆ Some rooms en-suite
6 £15
Self-catering accommodation also
available at £295/week ★★★★

ST LEONARDS

SP9107 0.9 miles (1.5km)
Wendover 3 miles (5km) C

Pub: White Lion 01494 758387

Field Cottage *closed Xmas & New Year*
Mrs Sue Jepson
St Leonards, Tring HP23 6NS
T: 01494 837602 **F:** 01494 837137
E: michael.jepson@lineone.net
www.smoothhound.co.uk/hotels/
field.html
1 £65 1 £65 (£50) 1 £40
✝✝ (min age 12) V DRY
◆◆◆ Some rooms en-suite
VisitBritain Silver Award

WIGGINTON

SP9310 on path
Tring 1 miles (2km) C

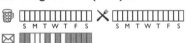

☆ Tring Park
www.tring.gov.uk/info/tpark.htm

Rangers Cottage
Mrs Sally Dawson
Tring Park, Wigginton, Tring HP23 6EB
T: 01442 890155 **F:** 01442 827814
E: rangerscottage@aol.com
www.rangerscottage.com
2 £65 1 £65 (£55) ✝✝ V
DRY Mastercard, Visa ◆◆◆◆
All rooms en-suite

The Greyhound Inn

Ms Sue Bickerdike
Chesham Road, Wigginton HP23 6EH
T: 01442 824631
www.the-greyhound.co.uk
🛏 2 £65 🛏 1 £75 (£50) 🚭 ♿ ♿
V 🅥 💳 Visa, Mastercard, Delta. All
rooms en-suite

TRING

➤ **SP9211** 🥾 1.2 miles (2km)
🚂 Tring ℹ️

Small town with full range of services,
visit www.tring.gov.uk for further
details. It has a good range of
accommodation and details can be
obtained from the Tourist Information
Centre - details in the introduction
section.

☆ The Walter Rothschild Zoological
Museum
T: 0207 9426171
www.nhm.ac.uk/visit-us/galleries/tring

☆ Grand Union Canal
www.waterscape.com/
Grand_Union_Canal

☆ Duchies Piece Nature Reserve
www.wildlifetrust.org.uk/herts/reserves

ALDBURY

➤ **SP9612** 🥾 0.6 miles (1km)
🚂 Tring 1 miles (1.5km) 📞

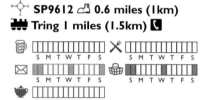

Pubs: Greyhound 01442 851228 &
Valiant Trooper 01442 851203

☆ Ashridge Estate
T: 01494 755557
www.nationaltrust.org.uk

16 Stoneycroft　　　*closed Xmas*

Mrs Sandra Crannage
Aldbury, Tring HP23 5RL
T: 01442 851294 **M:** 07801 846351
F: 01442 851294
🛏 1 £45 🛏 1 £45 (£22) 🚭 ♿ 🏠
V ♿ 🚲 DRY 🚗 🎒

The Greyhound Inn

Mr Tim O'Gorman
Aldbury, Tring HP23 5RT
T: 01442 851228 **F:** 01442 851495
www.greyhoundaldbury.co.uk
🛏 8 £75 (£65) 🚭 ♿ ♿ 🏠 V ♿ 🅥
🚲 🎒 💳 Mastercard, Visa, Delta. All
rooms en-suite

PITSTONE

SP9315 1.6 miles (2.5km)
Tring 2 miles (4km)

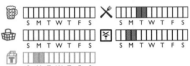

Pubs: Bell 01296 668078 & Duke of
Wellington 01296 661402

☆ Pitstone Windmill
www.nationaltrust.org.uk

☆ Pitstone Green Museum
T: 01494 528051
http://website.lineone.net/~pitstonemus

IVINGHOE

SP9416 0.9 miles (1.5km)
Tring 3 miles (5km)

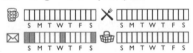

☆ Ford End Water Mill

Violets

Town Farm — SC

GR SP950164 0.9 miles (1.4km)
from Ridgeway
Mrs Leach
Ivinghoe, Leighton Buzzard LU7 9EL
T: 01296 660279 **M:** 07984 418914
F: 01296 662836
E: info@letsunlimited.com
www.letsunlimited.com

Mastercard, Visa, American Express,
Delta ★★★
1 bedroom and 3 bedroom cottages
available for holiday let

YHA Ivinghoe — SC

Mr Tim Martin
Old Brewery House, 3 High Street,
Ivinghoe LU7 9EP
T: 0870 7705884 **F:** 0870 7705885
E: ivinghoe@yha.org.uk
www.yha.org.uk

4 £60 3 £18 Mastercard, Visa, Delta,
Solo, Switch ★ Some rooms en-suite
Single beds are in shared dormitory.
Self-catering from £13.95/adult

The Silver Birch Campsite
closed 1 Dec - 31 March

Mrs Jane Rance
Upper Icknield Way, Ivinghoe, Leighton
Buzzard LU7 9EN
T: 01296 668348 **M:** 07760 491880
10 £3/person WC

EDLESBOROUGH

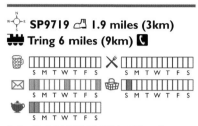

SP9719 👟 **1.9 miles (3km)**

🚂 **Tring 6 miles (9km)** 📞

🍳	S M T W T F S	✗	S M T W T F S
✉	S M T W T F S	🧺	S M T W T F S
🍺	S M T W T F S

Pubs: Bell 01525 220314 & Travellers
Rest 01525 221841

Ridgeway End   *closed Xmas*

Mrs Judith Lloyd
5 Ivinghoe Way, Edlesborough,
Dunstable LU6 2EL
T: 01525 220405 **M:** 07721 027339
F: 01525 220405
E: judy.lloyd@tesco.net
🛏 1 £48   1 £48   1 £50 (£30)
🚭 👫 V 🏇 🚴 **DRY** 🚗 👣
All rooms en-suite

Near Ivinghoe Beacon

Aldbourne 46
Aldbury................................ 91
Aldworth 62
Ardington............................ 59
Ashbury 48
Askett 85
Aston Rowant...................... 82
Avebury 36
Barbury Castle 37
Bishopstone......................... 47
Bledlow............................... 84
Blewbury 62
Britwell Salome.................... 75
Broad Hinton 37
Butlers Cross 86
Chilton 61
Chinnor 83
Chiseldon 38
Christmas Common 81
Compton 61
Cookley Green..................... 75
Crowell............................... 83
Crowmarsh Gifford 72
East Hendred....................... 60
East Ilsley 61
East Kennett 36
Edlesborough....................... 93
Ewelme 75
Farnborough 59
Goring-on-Thames............... 71
Great Kimble....................... 86
Hailey 73
Henton 84
Ivinghoe.............................. 92
Kingston Blount 82
Kingston Lisle 50
Lee Common 90
Letcombe Regis 57
Lewknor 81

Liddington 46
Lockeridge 35
Lockinge 58
Lodge Hill 84
Loosley Row 84
Lower Cadsden.................... 85
Marlborough 35
Moulsford........................... 63
Nettlebed............................ 74
North Stoke 72
Nuffield 74
Ogbourne St George 39
Park Corner 75
Pitstone.............................. 92
Postcombe 81
Princes Risborough 85
St Leonards 90
Saunderton Lee.................... 84
South Stoke 71
Sparsholt............................ 50
Stokenchurch...................... 82
Streatley 64
Tring.................................. 91
Uffington............................ 48
Upton 61
Wallingford......................... 73
Wanborough 46
Wantage 58
Watlington 76
Wendover 86
West Hendred 59
West Ilsley 60
West Overton...................... 35
Whiteleaf 85
Wigginton........................... 90
Winterbourne Bassett 36
Winterbourne Monkton........ 36
Woolstone 48
Wroughton 37

Distances between places along The Ridgeway in miles

	Overton Hill	Ogbourne St George	Fox Hill	Uffington Castle	Sparsholt Firs	A338 (Wantage)	Bury Down	Streatley	Mongewell Park	Nuffield	Watlington	Chinnor	Princes Risborough	Wendover	Wigginton
Ogbourne St George	9.3														
Fox Hill	17.0	7.7													
Uffington Castle	22.3	13.0	5.3												
Sparsholt Firs	25.3	16.0	8.3	3.0											
A338 (Wantage)	29.1	19.8	12.1	6.8	3.8										
Bury Down	34.5	25.2	17.5	12.2	9.2	5.4									
Streatley	42.7	33.4	25.7	20.4	17.4	13.6	8.2								
Mongewell Park	48.5	39.2	31.5	26.2	23.2	19.4	14.0	5.8							
Nuffield	52.4	43.1	35.4	30.1	27.1	23.3	17.9	9.7	3.9						
Watlington	58.0	48.7	41.0	35.7	32.7	28.9	23.5	15.3	9.5	5.6					
Chinnor	63.7	54.4	46.7	41.4	38.4	34.6	29.2	21.0	15.2	11.3	5.7				
Princes Risborough	68.5	59.2	51.5	46.2	43.2	39.4	34.0	25.8	20.0	16.1	10.5	4.8			
Wendover	75.0	65.7	58.0	52.7	49.7	45.9	40.5	32.3	26.5	22.6	17.0	11.3	6.5		
Wigginton	81.5	72.2	64.5	59.2	56.2	52.4	47.0	38.8	33.0	29.1	23.5	17.8	13.0	6.5	
Ivinghoe Beacon	86.8	77.5	69.8	64.5	61.5	57.7	52.3	44.1	38.3	34.4	28.8	23.1	18.3	11.8	5.3

Ivinghoe Beacon from Pitstone Hill